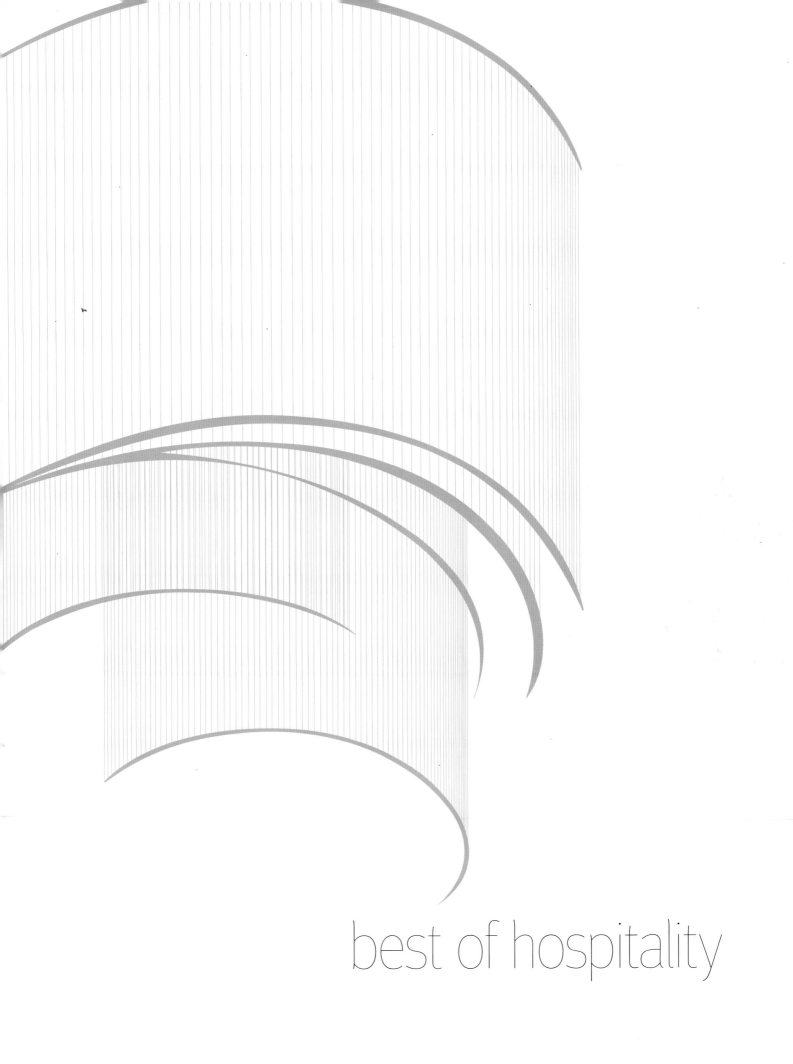

best of hospitality

INTERIOR DESIGN BEST OF HOSPITALITY

EDITOR IN CHIEF
Cindy Allen

EXECUTIVE EDITOR
Jen Renzi

SENIOR DESIGNER
Karla Lima

DESIGNERS
Selena Chen
Zigeng Li
Giannina Macias

EDITOR
Kathryn Daniels

MANAGING EDITOR
Helene E. Oberman

CONTRIBUTING WRITERS
Craig Kellogg
Julie Taraska
Stephen Treffinger
Athena Waligore

DIGITAL IMAGING
Igor Tsiperson

PRODUCTION
Sarah Dentry

BOOKS DIRECTOR
Selina Yee

TRAFFIC MANAGER
Kevin Cristaldi

PROJECT MANAGER
Kay Kojima

MARKETING DIRECTOR
Tina Brennan

MARKETING ART DIRECTOR
Denise Figueroa

Library of Congress Control Number 2011932699
ISBN-13: 978-0-9833263-1-1
ISBN-10: 0-9833263-1-2
Printed in China
10 9 8 7 6 5 4 3 2 1

INTERIOR DESIGN®

INTERIOR DESIGN MAGAZINE
360 Park Avenue South, 17th Floor, New York, NY 10010
www.interiordesign.net

SANDOW MEDIA LLC
Corporate Headquarters
3731 NW 8th Avenue, Boca Raton, FL 33431 www.sandowmedia.com

foreword
by Cindy Allen

Ask interior designers or architects what their dream commission would be, and invariably the answer is: "Hospitality, of course!" The allure of designing quintessentially intimate spaces joined to high-traffic gateways is simply irresistible to any creative firm. Ditto for the challenge of scaling it all up, often city blocks long, or down, to a tiny guest room.

We couldn't resist either. I'm delighted, therefore, to present the first volume in what will be an annual series of books, *Interior Design Best of Hospitality.* In these pages, you will see what boundless imagination and enormous commitment can do. The result is a rich portfolio of, count 'em, 71 projects by 41 of the world's brightest design stars—both the newly emerging and the long-established who continue to produce unparalleled fresh work. Through the force of their genius, they have set new standards, reenergizing the market and transforming it forever.

A shout-out to three of *Interior Design*'s hospitality Giants firms, universally respected and very present in this portfolio. For more than a decade, the number-one on our list, HBA/Hirsch Bedner Associates, has led the charge. Hall of Fame member David Rockwell of the Rockwell Group, at number six, is named year after year by his peers as one of the most admired. And fairly new to the hospitality scene but already making her mark, racking up awards and commissions, is number 66, Lauren Rottet of Rottet Studio. In total, there are 11 hospitality Giants featured among these pages, but also represented are other big talents of all sizes, some of whom you will meet for the first time.

Where in the world do these titans ply their trade? Asia, particularly China, continues its boom, while activity in the Middle East has cooled down compared to three years prior. On the U.S. front, the South and Northeast are offering the greatest potential, with the West Coast and the Midwest next in line. Hot spots may change, but one thing remains clear. Hospitality provides designers an unprecedented opportunity to test their mettle, to put their unique imprimatur on a vast space and craft a holistic experience for the people who visit.

So, after you've read in these pages about all the glories out there, I ask you: *What will be your next hospitality design destination?*

best of hospitality
contents

domestic hotel

Designers of American hotels—boutique and otherwise—are often tasked with creating a home-away-from-home mis-en-scène.

Visitors want to feel relaxed and welcomed, and touches like residentially appointed guest quarters, living room–esque lounge areas, and public spaces disguised as downtown lofts, prewar brownstones, or modernist glass boxes go a long way in accomplishing that goal. So does installing a curated collection of contemporary artworks (in one instance, executed by the designer himself). But half the fun of travel is *getting away*, a notion that leads designers to conjure a certain level of psychedelia, flamboyance, and full-on spectacle. Old Hollywood glamour is often a reference point (consider one hotel's red-carpet entrance) and a means to broadcast silver-screen chic—and help guests transcend the quotidien. Anything can happen on the road, even a romantic rendezvous over martinis in a three-story crystal chandelier (!). *Check in—and check it out.*

THE SURREY, NEW YORK

Discreet service in an intimate, upscale setting has been the hallmark of the Surrey since 1926, when it opened as a residential hotel. Over the years, this Upper East Side jewel has served as home to such notables as Bette Davis, JFK, and Claudette Colbert, and today it offers its clientele rare charm and formal elegance.

A recent remodeling by Lauren Rottet was inspired by a pedigreed New York City townhouse passed down through the generations. Most guest-room furniture is custom but has an heirloom feel, as if it were collected over many decades. The entry—kitted out in an old-world mélange of limestone, marble, crown moldings, and leaded glass—is also enhanced with contemporary touches like provocative artworks and a mosaic with a Surrealist, skewed pattern modeled on an Aubusson rug. A hidden rooftop garden is manicured in a French style, casually though intentionally allowed to run a bit wild.

Guests can wind down in the elegant yet warm Art Deco—style bar, with walls cocooned in quilted beige suede and banquettes upholstered in leather. Handpainted numbers on the barstools create a cheeky sense of organization, while the carpet is embellished with a poem, as if speaking in verse to patrons. It's the perfectly subtle, rich atmosphere for a modern-day rendezvous.

From top: Near the main lobby, a Chuck Close tapestry of Kate Moss presides over a hallway clad in statuary white, gray Bardiglio, and black Zimbabwean marble; steel-frame mirrors abut a wall of French limestone. Numbers sketched by Rottet were painted by Jimmie Martin on the custom stainless-steel barstools' leather backs. ➤

Rottet Studio

$60 million+ budget
189 guest rooms and 32 suites

Clockwise from left:
In the penthouse suite, a custom mohair sofa sits on a rug with a lacy border; the photograph is by architect Amy Sims. A bedside lamp in the airy presidential suite is a custom design in glass and polished nickel, with a linen shade. Painted aluminum and steel frame the entry canopy. In one of the presidential suite's two bathrooms, marble surfaces include a floor mosaic of a Surrey logo. The lobby's faux rug is rendered in marble tesserae.

PROJECT TEAM LAUREN ROTTET, DAVID DAVIS, RICHARD RIVEIRE, CHRISTOPHER OLEXY, CHRIS EVANS, LAURENCE CARTLEDGE

PHOTOGRAPHY ERIC LAIGNEL

www.rottetstudio.com

1 ELEVATOR LOBBY

2 STANDARD GUEST ROOM

3 SUITE

W HOLLYWOOD HOTEL & RESIDENCES
+ DRAI'S HOLLYWOOD, CALIFORNIA

Designstudio Ltd

Silver-screen style and SoCal modernism co-star in the design of this boutique property at the corner of Hollywood and Vine. Guests get the celebrity treatment from the moment they step onto the entry promenade, where a red carpet ushers them inside. There, the catwalk leads past reception to a spiral staircase, ringed with mirrored panels, that ascends from the lobby lounge to the second-floor amenities. Touches of crimson recur throughout, from the facade's logo to poolside chaise longues the color of maraschino cherries. Shades of green inform the palette, too: The building is currently the largest LEED-certified project in Southern California.

Sustainable cred aside, the interiors are resolutely glam. Twinkly crystal chandeliers form dramatic centerpieces. Full-height glass walls dissolving boundaries between inside and out add a dose of Midcentury mod. And guest rooms feature a confection of glossy white furnishings, furry throws, and snakeskin pillows that could have been plucked from the set of a futuristic '60s flick.

The penthouse floor houses Drai's Hollywood, a 20,000-square-foot rooftop club conceived with a French parlor in mind: Red-velvet drapes back a series of banquettes dressed in metallic-glazed leather; bronze-mirrored columns lend more shimmer; and the DJ booth is set off by a massive gold-leaf picture frame. Drai's isn't the only space catering to VIPs, either: Full floors of guest quarters can be reconfigured to accommodate film-premiere press junkets.

Clockwise from top left: The building logo, in the hotel's signature red. Casual groupings of low, backless lounges and poufs establish a languorous vibe in the Upper Living Room promenade. At the base of the spiral staircase, which rises over a river-rock moat, a round ottoman is illuminated by an LED-lit crystal chandelier. Limestone clads the rooftop pool deck, inspired by a Moroccan courtyard; above, VIP cabanas curtained with billowing drapes are accessed by a jasmine-lined staircase. ➤

0 10 20 40

1 RED CARPET

2 RECEPTION

3 LIVING ROOM

4 BAR

5 STAIRCASE

6 RETAIL

7 PROMENADE

8 STATION HOLLYWOOD

9 MTA PORTAL

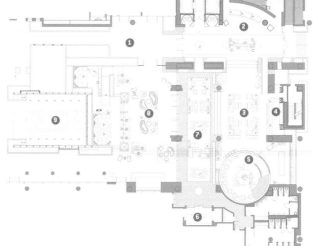

305 guest rooms and 150 residences
$350,000,000 (total project budget)
The Living Room lounge, Station Hollywood bar,
meeting spaces, rooftop pool and nightclub, and
outdoor bar with 20-foot-wide movie screen

PROJECT TEAM SHARILYN OLSON RIGDON, ANDREA ARRIOLA, CLIFFORD HEABERLIN, ROSE MARY GARRELS

ARCHITECTS OF RECORD HOTEL: HKS ARCHITECTS. DRAI'S: LEE & SAKAHARA ARCHITECTS

PHOTOGRAPHY ERIC LAIGNEL

www.designstudiolimited.com

Clockwise from opposite top: Boxy seating plays off otherwise curvaceous elements in the lobby-level Living Room; local houses by Frank Lloyd Wright inspired the bar's concrete-block screen. Semi-circular booths upholstered in gold- and silver-glazed leather line a window wall in Drai's Hollywood. Also at Drai's, a crystal chandelier, button-tufted sofa, and burgundy walls lend louche glamour. In a Marvelous Suite, sheers veil a custom seating unit below an etched-glass globe. A sinuous seating unit in the Extreme Wow Suite parlor.

TonyChi and Associates

ANDAZ 5TH AVENUE, NEW YORK

Across Fifth Avenue from this unique hotel are two city institutions: the New York Public Library flagship, a Beaux-Arts masterpiece whose famed lions flank the marble steps, and beyond that, a triumph of urban renewal—Bryant Park. Housed in a completely reconfigured former garment-industry building at 41st Street, the Andaz was intended to be, like the library and the park, a symbol of welcome, openness, and thought. Tony Chi achieved that aim via quiet, timeless interiors that rely on unfussy materials—blackened steel, white lacquer, mineralized oak, reclaimed brick, basalt—and a prewar aesthetic that lends the space the air of a turn-of-the-century Manhattan apartment.

Because every residence needs a library, there is the East Hall, a book nook near the entry. Eating and drinking is encouraged alongside reading: Besides bookshelves—whose rotating contents NYPL staff curates—and tables, the space boasts concealed refrigerators, a coffee station, a self-serve pantry, and a bar. Other public areas on the ground level have a similarly domestic vibe, with spare but comfortable vignettes for lounging, interacting, and making yourself at home.

The entire second floor, called Apartment 2E, is reserved for events. It has three studios and its own kitchen, and the malleable spaces can be tailored to the occasion and party size. Speaking of studios, guest accommodations have the ambience of ethereal loft apartments, with hardwood floors, luxuriously deep lounges, and a black-and-white palette that's quintessential New York.

From top: A glimpse of the library, seen through the entry pavilion's steel-framed sash windows. In the West Hall, small gatherings (up to eight people) take place at a walnut tasting table; a painting by Carlos Capelan disguises doors that pivot open to a lounge. Scored limestone frames the facade's delicately etched bronze transom panels, crafted by artist Christian Heckscher. ➤

184 guest rooms
46 seats (restaurant)
Gallery retail space, event space, gym, and cellar tavern with cheese cave

Clockwise from top: A massive soaking tub invites a deep steep in a Splash Suite. A row of black-washed poplar shutters allows the kitchen to be open or closed to the Shop restaurant, where wine storage also acts as a privacy screen. The glassed-in kitchen of Apartment 2E is visible through one of the property's many lacquered portals. The Den features a wine-storage wall, linen sofas, and Deirdre Jordan burled-walnut chairs, handmade by Amish craftsmen; wall moldings were designed to recall a prewar Manhattan apartment. Guest-room seating areas have hardwood floors and residentially appointed furnishings.

PROJECT TEAM TONY CHI, WILLIAM PALEY, NELSON BICOL, JOHNNY MARSH

LIGHTING CONSULTANT ARCLIGHT

GRAPHIC DESIGN LOUEY RUBINO DESIGN

PHOTOGRAPHY NIKOLAS KOENIG/COURTESY OF ANDAZ 5TH AVENUE

www.tonychi.com

```
0    10    20         40
```

1 ENTRY

2 LIBRARY

3 EAST HALL LOUNGE

4 DEN

5 WEST HALL LOUNGE

6 THE SHOP

7 KITCHEN

Rockwell Group

THE COSMOPOLITAN OF LAS VEGAS

In a city that's known for flamboyant gestures, this high-octane urban resort on the Strip stands out for its bevy of superlatives. The sprawling property boasts 2,995 oversize guest rooms spread between two 50-story towers, 150,000 square feet of convention and banquet facilities, a 50,000-square-foot spa, three pools, a fanciful casino, and a three-story walk-in chandelier (yes, you heard that right).

Despite said vastness, the Cosmopolitan feels unexpectedly intimate, even boutique-y, thanks to the firm's attention to detail and efforts to break down the amped-up scale of the interiors. The west lobby, for instance, features an enfilade of eight freestanding registration desks in lieu of one long counter. And the standard rooms, suites, and three-story poolside "bungalows" boast residential touches like button-tufted settees, sycamore-clad galley kitchens, Japanese soaking tubs, and Piero Fornasetti wallpaper.

As inviting as the guest quarters are, it would be a shame to spend all your time cocooned inside when so many amenities (and such great nightlife) beckon in this edgy adult playground. The resort includes 13 restaurants, serviced by a single gathering space, P3 Commons, whose eclectic seating groups are topped by a swirling stained-glass ceiling. Among the most popular dining destinations is Jaleo, whose vibrant Spanish-theme decor (Jaime Hayón dining chairs, faux bull's-head taxidermy, and the like) is a nod to chef José Andrés's native country.

Spend your slot-machine spoils at the casino's triple-level Chandelier bar. Its walls are sparkling curtains composed of more than 2 million crystal beads—the largest installation in North America. In this case, it's too bad that what happens in Vegas stays in Vegas, because we could all use some of that glitter in our everyday lives.

Clockwise from opposite top: In the granite-floored main lobby, which features a mirrored ceiling, structural columns are clad in LCD screens; visible at the rear are two of the antique-inspired reception desks. At Jaleo, a bull "trophy" by Mikel Urmeneta joins pendant fixtures by Jordi Vilardelo and chairs by Lievore Altherr Molina. In the restaurant's library-theme private dining room, Martí Guixé lighting hangs above chairs (by Hayón Studio) and a custom table topped with black walnut. Guests can take a dip in the hotel's three pools.

2,995 guest rooms
219 seats (Jaleo)
Nightclub, ultra lounge, convention and banquet facilities, 13 restaurants, spa, salon and fitness center, retail, and 3 pools

PROJECT TEAM ROCKWELL GROUP: DAVID ROCKWELL, EDMOND BAKOS, SHAWN SULLIVAN, DIEGO GRONDA, GREGORY STANFORD, ROBERT VERTES, MARTIN WEINER, HILLI WUERZ, BONNY BELLANT, KEVIN CAULFIELD , RAY CHUANG, JESSICA DAVENPORT, ANNE DUTERME, RAHM EREZ, LAUREN FARQUHAR, CHARLES FARRUGGIO, PENELOPE FISHER-WHITE, JULIE FRANK, HAROLD GAINER, PILAR GARCIA DE GONZALO, TOM HAGGERTY, ANDRE KIM, EMILY MORLEY, JODEL NARCISSE, GEORGE PRICE, JEAN-MARC TANG, NANCY THIEL, FABIOLA TRONCOSO. LAB: MELISSA HOFFMAN, JAMES TICHENOR, JOSHUA WALTON, TUCKER VIEMEISTER, LARS BERG, ZACK BOKA, JEFF CROUSE, KEETRA DIXON, ZACK GAGE, JAMES GEORGE, ELLEN HALLER, CALEB JOHNSTON, BRETT RENFER, DAN SAVAGE

PHOTOGRAPHY JAMES MEDCRAFT (1), JEFF GREEN (2, 3), COURTESY OF THE COSMOPOLITAN OF LAS VEGAS (4–7)

www.rockwellgroup.com

Clockwise from left:
Talk about over the top: Rising from the casino floor, the Chandelier bar is draped with Teflon-coated stainless-steel cables and miles of crystal beads. In the Commons, seating groups commingle such vintage pieces as a Midcentury sofa by Vladimir Kagan and a 1945 billiard table. An Elliott Erwitt photograph hangs near a suite's custom stained-walnut chairs and wraparound sofa.

1 HOST

2 BAR

3 STAGE

4 GLASS STAIR

5 GLASS ELEVATOR

0   10   20   40

10,000 sf
3 keys, 9 beds
Golf course, clubhouse, and heliport

Lindsay Newman Architecture and Design

LIBERTY NATIONAL GUEST HOUSE, JERSEY CITY, NEW JERSEY

From above: The guest house, viewed from the property's boat launch, is sliced by two projecting ipe-wood decks, whose bordering glass panels provide a buffer from the elements. In the entry lobby, sheers diffuse the abundant light while allowing colors and sights to show through impressionistically; support beams were strategically integrated into the interior design.

Plenty of golf courses tout spectacular mountain or ocean views, but only one can claim Lady Liberty stands within a thousand yards of the 18th green. For out-of-town members who prefer a little history with their travels, the by-invitation-only Liberty National golf club offers an unparalleled experience, both inside and out.

Even minus the stunning setting—on the Hudson River in Jersey City—the on-site guest house would qualify as a work of art. Within the ultramodern wood-and-glass arrangement of energetic lines and angles are three vast, full-floor apartments masterminded by interior designer Cat Lindsay and architect John Newman, who also oversaw the adjacent clubhouse.

The guest house has traveled a ways from its original intent—it was conceived as a restaurant with a two-story dining room. In the conversion, spaces were strategically divided to maximize the number of bedrooms: at the least, three per floor, each with a private bath. The designers relocated both the elevator and fire stairs for a more gracious entryway and greater space. Large, projecting ipe-wood decks with glass railings were built on the top two levels, and landscaping was added on the ground floor.

The guest rooms are largely neutral with pleasing pops of color; they're plush but still streamlined, each item chosen with care. The decks, accessible from all living areas and most bedrooms, provide enviable views of New York harbor.

And the 7,400-yard golf course isn't half bad either—if you can take your eyes off the scenery long enough to putt.

Clockwise from left:
The third-level dining area features a custom wenge table; a partial wall serves to distinguish it from the vestibule and living area. In the living area, judicious smatterings of red accent the earth-tone furnishings. The third-level kitchen is dominated by custom white-lacquer cabinetry. In the same apartment, a master bedroom with a custom wenge bench and dresser. ➤

1 TERRACE
2 ENTRY VESTIBULE
3 LIVING AREA
4 DINING AREA
5 KITCHEN
6 BEDROOM

0   10   20   40

This master bedroom on level 3 showcases a panoramic view of New York Harbor, which can be savored from the privacy of bed, chair, or deck. Complimentary launch service is available—or bring your own vessel and dock right outside. ➤

"The interior design is much like the perfect meal— a meticulous combination of warm and cool, smooth and textured, delicate and piquant"

—CAT LINDSAY

Clockwise from opposite: A master bath on level 3, with milk-glass walls and Thassos marble flooring. A teak accent wall and custom credenza— made with hot rolled steel—greets guests as they enter the apartment. The third-floor living area, viewed from the dining room, features custom seating anchored by a silk carpet.

PROJECT TEAM CAT LINDSAY, JOHN NEWMAN, MANI COLAKU, MICHELLE DROLLETTE, PATRICK HOYLE, KRISTINA HARROD

PHOTOGRAPHY CHRIS COOPER

www.lnarchitecture.com

JansonGoldstein

ANDAZ WEST
HOLLYWOOD,
LOS ANGELES

Located in the heart of the Sunset Strip, this recently rehabbed hotel has a hard-partying past. Built in 1963, it was a crash pad favored by Robert Plant, Jim Morrison, and other rock-and-roll greats with a penchant for guitar smashing and guest-suite trashing, thus earning it the nickname the Riot House.

Hired to convert the structure into the first U.S. location of Hyatt's boutique-hotel spin-off, principal Hal Goldstein was guided by another Midcentury cultural phenomenon: L.A. modernist architecture, in particular the glass-box Case Study Houses. To give the dowdy building a facelift, he glazed the south-facing exposure, including guest-room balconies now enclosed in full-height windows to maximize square footage and sweeping views of the Hollywood Hills. The architect also revitalized the street-front presence by building a steel-frame glass pavilion to house RH, the hotel's bar and restaurant. Its facade presses right up against the Strip, offering diners a front-row view of nightlife parading by, as well as artist Jacob Hashimoto's installation of trippy metal hexagons.

Interiors are a similar mash-up of sleek finishes and vintage-inspired art. Glass pendants and lamps illuminate the loungelike lobby, anchored by a psychedelic backlit mural. A textured-metal screen behind the bar lends a groovy aura. The restaurant's biomorphic mosaic floor, which recalls the landscape designs of late Brazilian modernist Roberto Burle Marx, mimics a '60s pattern by sculptor Erwin Hauer. Its rebirth complete, the hotel has gone from Riot House to art house.

Clockwise from left:
Jacob Hashimoto's 11-foot-tall art installation is made of handpainted metal disks suspended from stainless-steel cables. Sheers curtain off the dining area of RH, which shares a glass wall with a wine display. Behind the marble-top bar is a screen of stamped stainless-steel tiles. The staircase leading from the lobby to the mezzanine-level meeting rooms has bronze-glass treads; the same material covers the platform below. ➤

180,000 sf
260 rooms
Rooftop terrace and pool

Clockwise from opposite top: The rooftop lounge overlooks downtown Los Angeles. RH's custom mosaic floor is tumbled Calacatta marble. Carrera marble tops the restaurant's communal tables. In the lobby lounge, a photographic mural lit from behind backs the reception desk.

PROJECT TEAM HAL GOLDSTEIN, MATTHEW JASION, CHIE IKEDA, VICTORIA NADY, MARY POLITES

ARCHITECT OF RECORD SCHLEMMER + ALGAZE + ASSOCIATES

PHOTOGRAPHY MIKIKO KIKUYAMA

www.jansongoldstein.com

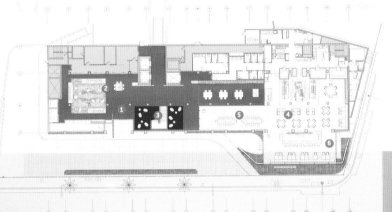

1 ENTRY

2 LOBBY LOUNGE

3 STAIRCASE

4 MAIN DINING

5 COMMUNAL TABLES

6 BAR

SUNSET BOULEVARD

FOUR SEASONS SEATTLE

BraytonHughes Design Studios

As the mantra goes, it's all about location, location, location. Of course, a superior design helps, too. This five-star property offers both in spades. Situated near the historic Pike Place Market and the Seattle Art Museum, the hotel commands drop-dead views of Elliott Bay and Puget Sound. Also conveniently close to the downtown financial district, it is ideally sited to lure the corporate jet-setters who make up a majority of the city's upscale travelers. The building's proximity to the waterfront, mountains, and urban grid sparked BHD's refined scheme, a breezy synthesis of Far East and Pacific Northwest styles.

Primary materials reflect the earthy, Japanese-modern sensibility. In public areas, lightly figured sycamore and ash commingle with muted stones of varying hues, sheens, and textures. The lobby is sheathed in soft greige stones, arrayed in a linear composition inspired by granite formations in the nearby Olympic Mountains. The crisp pattern of staggered lines continues in the adjacent restaurant and bar; striped wall, floor, and ceiling treatments lend rigor to the organic palette.

Guest quarters emphasize Zen-like comfort with luxe textiles dressing plush lounge chairs, beds, and supersize headboards. A medley of soft-spoken hues, accented by pale woods, shifts from suite to suite. These restful retreats summarize the vibe: sophisticated, serene, soulful.

Clockwise from top: A floating stairway ascends from the lobby to the function rooms; the walls and floor are treated to a quarrylike pattern of stone planks. Near Café Blue's exhibition-style prep area is a feature wall of backlit marble planks installed at varying intervals. Oversize upholstered headboards, sedate colorways, and built-in blond-wood storage units distinguish a guest room. ➹

147 guest rooms
Restaurant and bar, spa with fitness center and
outdoor pool, ballroom, and meeting room/
conference space

Clockwise from left: Near reception, seating vignettes are warmed by a focal fireplace; the abstract canvases are by prominent Seattle artists. The waiting area of the third-floor spa features tranquil colors and natural materials. Calacatta Gold marble clads the vanity and soaking tub of a guest-room bath.

1 HOTEL LOBBY

2 RESIDENTIAL LOBBY

3 FRONT DESK

4 RESTAURANT

5 BAR

6 RETAIL

0 10 20   40

PROJECT TEAM BRAYTONHUGHES DESIGN STUDIOS: RICHARD BRAYTON, KRIS KAWAII TORAL, ART CHEN, MEGHAN LOPEZ. NBBJ: LOUISA CHANG, JIM TULLY, NICK CHARLES, BRUCE GABERT, KERRY HEGEDUS

PHOTOGRAPHY BEN BENSCHNEIDER

www.bhdstudios.com

GoodmanCharlton

THE MODERNE HOTEL, NEW YORK

Clockwise from top: The facade, recently updated with aluminum paint. A hooded armchair upholstered in faux leather marks the elevator lobby in an upstairs corridor. In the parlor lounge, chesterfield sofas are complemented by designer Jeffrey Goodman's painting in the style of Franz Kline. The lounge's black-and-white decor is accented with tomato red in the form of throw pillows, a Global Views vase, and blooms by couture florist Hervé Gambs. A guest room has original arched window openings, a nailhead-studded sofa, and another piece by Goodman. ➘

Hired to put the "mod" back into the Moderne Hotel on West 55th Street, Jeffrey Goodman and Steven Charlton turned to Midcentury art for guidance. (Considering MoMA is just a few blocks away, they didn't have to go far for inspiration.) As a paean to Andy Warhol's Factory, the designers treated the facade to a slick of aluminum paint. Metallic touches shimmer inside, too, from the parlor's silver chesterfield sofas to guest-room desk chairs. The duo commissioned a colorful mural from New York painter Malcolm Hill for the wood-paneled lobby; the best spot from which to appreciate the geometric frieze is a black patent-leather armchair below. Nearby, a vintage Curtis Jere sculpture hangs against a chimney of split-face quartzite. Hallways are papered in a vivid custom print depicting a salon-style installation of empty picture frames. Completing the blue-chip theme, Goodman peppered the interiors with canvases he painted in the style of Abstract Expressionists Helen Frankenthaler, Franz Kline, and Morris Louis.

Influenced by the European tradition of converting old homes into jewel-box hotels, the firm also reworked the 19th-century brownstone to take better advantage of its intimate scale. That explains such residential touches as a new terrace and roof garden, a common living parlor, and guest rooms opened up for a more expansive feel. The upshot? A sense you're crashing in the townhouse of a private art-collector friend.

34 guest rooms
6 months from
concept to installation

Clockwise from opposite top: In the living parlor, a split-face quartzite hearth frames a gas fireplace. The color of the handscreened wallpaper animating corridors changes from floor to floor. Custom patent-leather armchairs await below Malcolm Hill's handpainted frieze in the wood-clad lobby. Oly zebra-print pillows dress up a guest room's tufted-leather bed. The faux bois broadloom is custom.

PROJECT TEAM JEFFREY GOODMAN, STEVEN CHARLTON
PHOTOGRAPHY DYLAN PATRICK PHOTOGRAPHY
www.goodmancharlton.com

Stephen B. Jacobs Group/ Andi Pepper Interior Design

GANSEVOORT PARK HOTEL, NEW YORK

Rising from the corner of Park Avenue South and 29th Street in Manhattan, this 18-story boutique hotel has a downtown vibe and a chameleonic nature. By day, its honed and polished granite exterior blends in with the neighboring buildings. In the evening, the facade lights up with a rainbow-hued LED show, hinting at the property's colorful personality.

Step inside and you'll see: The triple-height lobby's neutral backdrop is perked up with oversize aubergine chandeliers. Calm-toned guest rooms with comfortable seating and work areas are punctuated with vibrant artwork, fuchsia window treatments, and lavender accent chairs. Bathrooms, meanwhile, are soothing and spalike, with sand-hued glass-tile walls, trough sinks, and soaking tubs. Even more luxurious is the duplex presidential suite, boasting a two-story living room and a sheltered outdoor terrace.

The hotel's top three floors are designed for maximum flexibility, consisting of four adjacent spaces that can function as separate VIP/event rooms or be combined to host one giant bar scene. There's a fluidity between indoors and out, dramatically expressed on the exterior. A cantilevered corner balcony with glass openings not only allows patrons to look out but also invites pedestrians to observe the action inside—taking the rooftop bar to a whole new level.

Clockwise from above: The lobby, lit by a series of glass chandeliers, welcomes patrons with black-and-white chevron-patterned granite floors and herringbone-print chairs. A 150-foot-tall LED-lit glass column brightens the building's corner. A heated outdoor pool offers clear sight lines to the Empire State Building. The mermaid-theme Blue Room bar is part of the triplex roof complex. ➥

197,000 sf
$102,000,000 budget
249 keys

PROJECT TEAM STEPHEN B. JACOBS GROUP: STEPHEN B. JACOBS,
HERBERT E. WEBER JR., ISAAC-DANIEL ASTRACHAN, RICKY ENG.
ANDI PEPPER INTERIOR DESIGN: ANDI PEPPER, MAYA PARKHANI

PHOTOGRAPHY MAGDA BIERNAT (1, 4, 8), ALEX SEVERIN (2, 3), WOODRUFF BROWN (5–7)

www.sbjgroup.com

```
0    5    10        20
```

1 LIVING AREA

2 DINING AREA

3 TERRACE

4 BEDROOM

Clockwise from top: *Generously proportioned corner suites offer four-poster beds, multitasking work areas, and spicy artwork. The presidential suite's double-height living area, decked out in color-accented earth tones, has a spiral staircase leading to the master bedroom. Guest rooms' oversize bathrooms boast a separate tub and glass-enclosed shower. The rooftop bar is set against the glass facade, under a pair of custom chandeliers.*

275,000 sf
282 guest rooms and suites

SFA Design

FOUR SEASONS LOS ANGELES AT BEVERLY HILLS

Long a home away from home for film-industry moguls and upscale travelers alike, this property is famous for its power-breakfast scene. But even though scores of actors, rock stars, and movie execs still pass through its airy rooms on a daily basis, its traditional interiors sorely needed an update—the decor didn't quite align with the glamour of its clientele. SFA Design kept the flora-based aesthetic for which the chain is known, interweaving elements of Old Hollywood and Beverly Hills. By playing with scale, texture, finish, and color, the firm achieved a look that is clean and Southern California at its core...and decidedly more current than its previous iteration.

The 1940s silver-screen vibe is accomplished with mirrored coffee tables, lacquer finishes, and furniture bearing graceful curves. Layered onto that are more modern elements: flatscreen TVs, LED-lit crystal chandeliers, zebra-print upholstery fabrics, and silver-leaf elements.

Varying palettes were used for guest quarters. Luxury suites feature warm, chocolate-brown wood tones shot through with hints of ice blue and camel. In the Presidential Suite West, cream and black furnishings are accented with plum, celadon, and coral. The Presidential Suite East is more mod, with straighter lines and bold contemporary artworks. Ecru and brown dominate the living areas, while the den and master suite incorporate smoky gray and burnt caramel.

The refresh brings a dose of European elegance, yet at its heart the hotel remains très L.A.—a smart and zingy backdrop for star-studded drama.

From above: The nature theme is carried into a luxury suite's bedroom via an upholstered floral headboard wall. A hand-tufted butterfly carpet decorates the Presidential West Suite's living/dining area, where Tord Boontje's Blossom chandelier for Swarovski twinkles above a silver-leaf dining table. ⤳

1 ENTRY FOYER

2 FRONT DESK

3 LIBRARY

4 GARDEN SUITES

5 LOUNGE

6 CAFÉ

7 RESTAURANT

8 BALLROOM

9 LAWN

0   20   40   80

Clockwise from left:
Upholstery colors pick up the expansive carpet's hues in the living/dining area of the Presidential West Suite; a mirrored coffee table and glossy ceiling inset provide soft shimmer. The Presidential East Suite is more contemporary, with graphic dark-stained wood furnishings and assertive artworks. Both presidential suites offer in-room baby grands along with downtown views.

PROJECT TEAM SUE FIRESTONE, KARA SMITH
PHOTOGRAPHY DON RIDDLE
www.sfadesign.com

Daroff Design

Is a design capable of making guests feel welcome? In the case of this hotel, the answer is, resoundingly, yes. The firm's careful consideration of both the general and the particular is clear, from the column-free event spaces to the lofty bedding and doe-skin bathrobes in guest rooms. The brand claims comfort as its standard, and its luxury Atlanta property bears this out.

A sense of hushed drama prevails when one enters the lobby. Monumental, almost totemic, wenge-clad beams form a frame of sorts around the sleek stainless-steel reception desk. A white-on-white backdrop—a commissioned sculpture by local artist Marty Dawe— draws visitors with its intriguing glow.

The scheme celebrates the city's visual- and performing-arts culture. Details such as the lobby lounge's internally lit column covers—evocative of piano keys—and rich millwork nod to musical instruments. Muted lighting warms the entire scene, and punchy color injects energy into the otherwise restrained palette. The adjacent restaurant, Eleven, reiterates the soothing spirit. So do guest rooms, where espresso-hued finishes are accented with vibrant strokes of red.

Throughout the property, contrasts of neutral/bright, cool/warm, wood/marble, and quiet/bold work to create visual excitement while fostering restful comfort. The overall impression? Elegant yet energetic calm.

PROJECT TEAM KAREN DAROFF, ALINA JAKUBSKI, PIER DERRICKSON, JANEY GARRIDO, RICHARD LANNING

ARCHITECT OF RECORD RULE JOY TRAMMEL

PHOTOGRAPHY MICHAEL KLEINBERG

www.daroffdesign.com

34,000 sf (event space)
414 guest rooms

Clockwise from opposite top: *Bracketing the plush lounge lobby are "piano key" light fixtures. A guest suite with dark-stained wood furnishings and a full-height upholstered headboard. Eleven, the hotel's ground-floor restaurant, has hardwood floors and abstract art. The bar area, located off the lobby, centers around a striking bottle display. Sheers veil full-height city views in one of the presidential suites.*

Rockwell Group

AMES HOTEL, BOSTON

Constructed in 1893, the 13-story Ames Building was Boston's first skyscraper. So when Rockwell Group—working in conjunction with the property's operators, Morgans Hotel Group and Normandy Real Estate Partners—set about converting the 70,000-square-foot Richardson Romanesque structure into a luxury hotel and restaurant, the challenge was to preserve the landmark's history while smartening its interiors.

To that end, studio leader Gregory Stanford opted for sleek lines and a black-and-white palette accented with splashes of gray and cinnabar. The minimalist color scheme allows architectural details like the lobby's original barrel-vaulted ceiling to take center stage; it also provides a graphic backdrop to the numerous commissioned artworks,

including a delicate Mylar-and-wire chandelier by Sophie Nielsen and Rolf Knudsen that bewitches just inside the main entrance. The piece sets the tone for the hotel's 114 guest rooms and suites, residentially appointed aeries that feature 10-foot ceilings, lacquered furnishings, and natural light spilling through oversize windows curtained with full-height sheers.

Contrast that with the Woodward, the hotel's award-winning eatery. Cultivating a dandyish vibe, the moody two-story tavern features tailored leather banquettes, reclaimed teak flooring, and an 18-foot-bar that's ideal for an afternoon martini. Adorning the restaurant's upper level is a Victorian-inspired metal cabinet of curiosities, stocked with over 200 objets—an ever-changing collection of treasures handpicked by the designers.

Clockwise from above: Sophie Nielsen and Rolf Knudsen's Mirror Cloud glitters above the entry. Guest bathrooms boast Duravit vanities, porcelain floors, and white-marble walk-in showers. Loftlike guest rooms feature pale oak floors, a lacquered nightstand, and black-chrome fixtures modeled on antique whale-oil lamps. The living area of the ninth-floor apartment is furnished with a vintage tufted-velvet chaise and Moroso sofas; the pendant light in the dining area has a feather-clad drum shade. The monochrome lobby lounge's Matt Gagnon chandelier. The Woodward restaurant offers candlelit alcoves.

PROJECT TEAM ROCKWELL GROUP: DAVID ROCKWELL, GREGORY STANFORD, JESSICA DAVENPORT, CHARLES FARRUGGIO, FRANCES MONG. MORGANS HOTEL GROUP: MARI BALASTRAZZI, HEATHER MALONEY, TRACY SMITH

PHOTOGRAPHY COURTESY OF MORGANS HOTEL GROUP

www.rockwellgroup.com

275 sf (guest rooms)
1,050 sf (Celebrity Suite)
95 guest rooms, 12 suites,
5 hospitality suites, and 1 apartment

THE BEVERLY HILLS HOTEL, LOS ANGELES

Known as the Pink Palace for its distinctive tinted stuccowork, the Beverly Hills Hotel's Mediterranean Revival facade is every bit as iconic as the Hollywood sign. And so is its scene: Movie moguls and film stars have frequented this Sunset Boulevard landmark—a favorite spot for poolside power breakfasts—since its doors opened in 1912.

Catering to heads of state, royalty, and other illustrious patrons, two new presidential bungalows by Rottet Studio offer temporary private quarters on the hallowed—and lushly landscaped—grounds. Terracotta tile roofs, intimate gardens, and, yes, pink stucco exteriors acknowledge the past while touches like flatscreen TVs, fireplaces (five per bungalow), and remote-controlled lights provide the amenities modern guests demand.

Both bungalows feature gracefully freeflowing living-dining areas, as well as a den, plush study, three bedrooms, private plunge pool, and outdoor lounge areas. Hand-troweled Venetian-plaster walls, classic white moldings, distressed-walnut flooring, and other residential touches provide a serene backdrop for sculptural light fixtures, silk carpets, and '40s-inspired custom furniture distinguished by strong, graphic lines. Artworks by Claes Oldenburg and Larry Bell, meanwhile, bestow blue-chip grandeur. And contemporary stardom being what it is, closed-circuit cameras monitor all the comings and goings.

Clockwise from above: Burled-wood built-ins dominate the intimate study. A Claes Oldenburg print, Perfume Atomizer, on a Pillow on a Chair Leg, hangs in the living area, anchored by a silk rug—actually an art piece designed by Rottet Studio. A framed work by Larry Bell is mounted above the fireplace of a bedroom, which has access to a private garden. An elegant '40s-style vanity table furnishes the bathroom. The hotel's pink stucco exterior, visible near a private pool. Wallpaper with a Torrey-pine motif envelops a seating vignette in the den.

Rottet Studio

PROJECT TEAM LAUREN ROTTET, RICHARD RIVEIRE, MARK BORKOWSKI, LAURENCE CARTLEDGE
PHOTOGRAPHY FRED LICHT (1–4, 6), ERIC LAIGNEL (5)
www.rottetstudio.com

3,500 sf (per unit)
2 bungalows (6 keys)

375,000 sf
239 rooms

Bilkey Llinas Design

FOUR SEASONS HOTEL DENVER

Clockwise from above: Leather club chairs below glass pendants overlook the lobby's cantilevered stainless-steel staircase. The presidential suite's bathroom has both a rain showerhead and a freestanding tub with views of Denver. A double-sided fireplace divides the lobby and lounge. Warmed by a hearth and an earthy palette, the living area of the presidential suite commingles custom furnishings and contemporary artworks. A rustic slate-mosaic feature wall, rich wood cladding, and a wire sculpture distinguish the Edge restaurant.

The owner of this luxury hotel/condominium wanted to spike the native rusticity of wild Colorado with Mile High City chic. Thus urban modernist interiors are softened by materials relating in color and texture to the Rocky Mountains rising in the distance. Local flavor also comes in the form of the thousand-plus original artworks by area painters and sculptors, which lend a gallerylike feel.

The statement-making starts at the entry. Pressed right up against the glass facade of the 45-story mixed-use tower is a sculptural stainless-steel staircase with clear glass balustrades and marble treads. Giant steel sculptures by Jonathan Hils further highlight the entry sequence. Nearby, a monumental 17-foot-tall stone fireplace turns up the heat with a gas-fueled firebox enclosed in glass to permit views through dancing flames to the lobby lounge—and busy street—beyond. Wide floor planks laid diagonally impart subtle dynamism, while comfy leather armchairs cluster beneath a gaggle of pendant lanterns made with alabaster-toned milk glass.

Guest rooms and suites boast oversize windows that look out onto the mountain range; even the soaking tubs feature spectacular views. Amenities, however, are more inward-gazing: The spa offers circular whirlpool baths and a mosaic-lined pool conducive to quiet contemplation, while the Edge restaurant is a veritable bento box of high-touch textures and variegated finishes.

PROJECT TEAM ROBERT BILKEY, OSCAR LLINAS, MAURICIO SALCEDO, DENIS MULHERN, JUDE MULHERN, JOSE FERREIRA, JULIUS CRISTOBAL

DESIGN ARCHITECT CARNEY LOGAN BURKE ARCHITECTS

ARCHITECT OF RECORD HKS

PHOTOGRAPHY DON RIDDLE (1, 3), PETER VITALE (2, 4), LARA KASTNER (5)

www.bilkeyllinas.com

international hotel

The following properties span the globe, from Germany to Namibia. As aesthetically diverse as they are, the projects share a common sensibility: The design of each captures the unique character of its locale while rising above cultural clichés.

When regional motifs are called upon to telegraph a sense of place, they're abstracted, stylized, or otherwise tweaked into a wink-wink blend of old and new. Check out the Park Hyatt Istanbul's Iznik-tiled feature wall, Hilton Windhoek Plaza Hotel's scaled-up animal prints, and the decorative plasterwork in the Four Seasons Hotel London at Park Lane. Similarly witty riffs on vernacular elements distinguish the Chinese properties featured herein (rumors of the country's hospitality boom are not exaggerated), which inventively interpret Sung Dynasty design, Shikumen courtyard architecture, and other decorative strains. One trend that breaks with tradition but transcends national borders: the open-plan bathroom—a welcome novelty that's more prevalent abroad. *Soak it in.*

Istanbul's posh Nişantaşı neighborhood provides the backdrop for this stylish collision of historic and contemporary design. The Park Hyatt joins the Maçka Palas—a neoclassic structure built as an ambassador's residence in 1922—with the newer glass-and-steel Petit Palace, a converted car showroom. GKV oversaw the merger and renovation, which resulted in 85 glamorous guest rooms and five elegant penthouse suites, as well as a restaurant and rooftop bar.

"It's European opulence meets Agatha Christie's *Orient Express*," explains principal Randy Gerner. The expansive lobby's double-height feature wall reinterprets traditional—and typically colorful—Iznik tile in a tone-on-tone mosaic. A skylit walkway leads to the Maçka Palas, where guest rooms with touches of both Milanese palazzo and Art Deco style are situated. Accommodations average over 625 square feet, and many include extravagant wet rooms with Turkish baths, splash tubs, rain and steam showers, and color-therapy lighting. Speaking of illumination, guest quarters can be set in a choice of two dozen preprogrammed lighting schemes, from Work to Romantic to Sleep.

For dinner, Istanbul's very first steakhouse awaits, incorporating rich wood finishes, candlelit alcoves, and a red La Cornue–inspired stove in the central open kitchen. A wall is constructed of glass wine-storage boxes complete with high-tech cooling systems. The eatery deliberately references similar American restaurants—just the right "exotic" touch for a cosmopolitan setting.

Clockwise from below: The restored Italianate facade of the Maçka Palas. Modeled on traditional Iznik tilework, the lobby's two-story quartzite mosaic reflects the city's Byzantine and Ottoman pasts. In the steakhouse, a warm palette of dark-stained woods and chocolate-brown leathers combines with pale stone mosaics. Rich millwork defines a serene lounge. ➤

Gerner Kronick + Valcarcel, Architects

PARK HYATT ISTANBUL, MAÇKA PALAS, TURKEY

"East meeting West and yesterday meeting today: Those were our themes"
—RANDY GERNER

A limestone stairway lined with custom ottomans awaits guests in the hotel's minimalist entryway, located in the newer Petit Palace. The structural columns are veneered in crotch mahogany. ➤

Clockwise from far left: In a wet room with a "hammam corner," channel glass separates bathing and sleeping areas. Guest quarters feature 1950s black-and-white photographs. In another guest room, salvaged hickory floorboards combine with restored ceiling moldings; the custom chandelier is based on a 19th-century gas fixture. The lap pool's infinity edge is clad in iridescent mosaics.

160,600 sf
85 guest rooms and 5 penthouse suites

PROJECT TEAM BRYAN BENNETT, BERIL DEMIRCIOGLU, RIANA PIZZI, OZER ONKAL
PHOTOGRAPHY ERIC LAIGNEL
www.gkvarchitects.com

1 LIVING AREA

2 SLEEPING AREA

3 HAMMAM CORNER

4 BATHROOM

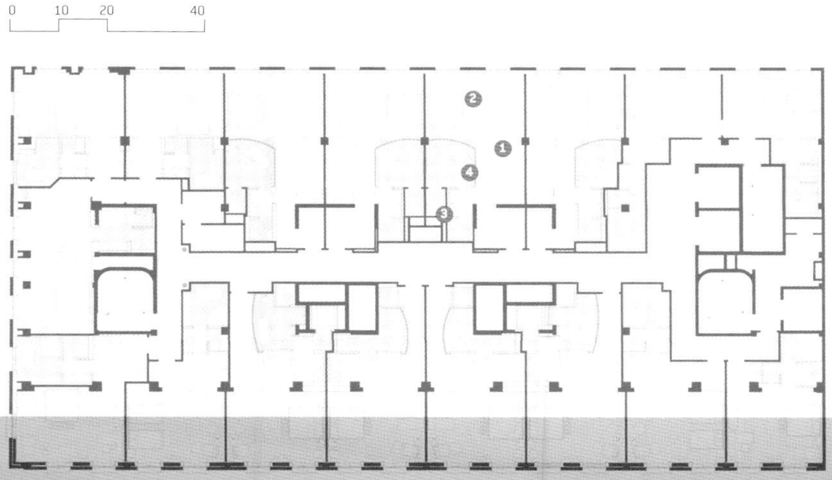

PYR

THE SAVOY, LONDON

Britain's first luxury hotel, the Savoy, opened in 1889, built with profits from Richard D'Oyly Carte's Gilbert & Sullivan opera company. Its unprecedented amenities included hot and cold running water, electric lights, and food by chef August Escoffier. For the recent renovation—a painstaking three-year process—PYR respected the hotel's history while adding modern elements and functionality.

Much effort was devoted to refurbishing the property's dramatic Edwardian and Art Deco details. Corinthian column capitals were regilded, ornate plasterwork was touched up, and the glass entry canopy—blacked out since World War II—was reglazed to admit sunlight. New finishes in both public and private areas are sympathetic with the period decor: black-and-white-checkerboard marble floors, dark-painted ceilings, Galaxy granite accents, gold-leaf and lizard wall treatments, and mahogany millwork. To leaven the drama, PYR threaded an airier palette of cream, light green, and pale rose throughout.

The hotel was also designed to establish a better connection with its surroundings. A Lalique crystal fountain now creates a more inviting entry sequence from the Strand, while the Grill takes better advantage of Thames views. So do river-facing Edwardian suites, dressed in a spectrum of soft hues that draw from English floral prints.

Some things, of course, remain unchanged: Here, Winston Churchill shared the daily afternoon meal with his cabinet. Today the Savoy continues the power-lunch tradition, with a new generation of notables.

Clockwise from top left: Arriving guests step into the main entry from a portico whose opaque canopy was replaced with glass to enhance natural illumination. In the Riverside restaurant, Deco style gets an update via rosewood furnishings, light sycamore woodwork, and upholstered wall panels and ceiling. Alcoves in the Beaufort bar are adorned in gold leaf. The bar itself, fashioned from backlit engraved glass, is set on a former opera stage.

Clockwise from opposite: *A new frosted-glass dome with multicolored frieze and metalwork gazebo, seen reflected in the Winter Garden's mirrored panels. Toile wall covering and paisley upholstery enlivens a cozy seating area in the Upper Thames lounge, a tea and chocolate salon. Another perspective on the expansive lobby, punctuated with tailored furniture groupings. An Art Deco suite's chromed brass sconce and sycamore nightstand, topped with black granite.*

268 guest rooms and suites
Restaurant, bar, two lounges, reading room, museum, and meeting rooms

PROJECT TEAM PIERRE-YVES ROCHON, ANNICK ROCHON, JEAN-MARIE HEIDERSCHEID, DANIEL JUGE, JENNY JOHNSON
ARCHITECT OF RECORD REARDON SMITH ARCHITECTS
PHOTOGRAPHY RICHARD BRYANT (1, 2, 4–8), NIALL CLUTTON (3)
www.pyr-design.com

PARK HYATT SHANGHAI, CHINA

TonyChi and Associates

For this tranquil property, the design team focused on creating a home away from home—albeit one situated near the top of the 101-story Shanghai World Financial Center. The hotel proper excludes loud bars and restaurants in favor of serene spaces, including a spa with a still infinity pool and tai chi area. Nodding to traditional Chinese courtyard architecture, public spaces flow together seamlessly to convey a residential feel. Likewise, small courtyards—instead of doors—connect guest rooms.

Tony Chi explains his goal: "To build silence," which is perhaps the greatest of luxuries in this populous metropolis. Accordingly, design elements emphasize a hushed drama. At ground level a succession of monastically spare chambers welcome guests; a tea salon recalls an elegant living room with round black tables and plush armchairs; and a bar's walls—and ceilings—are decadently swathed in green and tan leathers. Guest rooms extend the understated refinement, alternating between natural wood, honed stone, blackened furniture, and lacquer. A sense of calm is achieved through ceilings that soar 16 feet, walk-in dressing rooms, and entries that enhance privacy. You feel at home, although the vistas of Shanghai remind you that you are somewhere else entirely.

Clockwise from left:
The building entrance. In the hotel's main restaurant, high-back chairs are covered in cotton-linen; shagreen lines a wall and the flooring is walnut. Hand-chiseled Chinese granite and etched-bronze panels announce the ground-level approach sequence. ➤

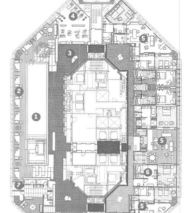

PHOTOGRAPHY MARC GERRITSEN (1), MICHAEL MORAN/OTTO (2–7)
www.tonychi.com

1 WATER'S EDGE
2 VERANDA
3 COURTYARD
4 GYM
5 SUITE
6 SPA TREATMENT AREA
7 STEAM ROOM
8 CHANGING AREAS

0   10   20   40

Clockwise from near right: *The bar's dramatic view. A tea salon in the 87th-floor lobby is outfitted with custom armchairs covered in linen and folding stools with leather seats, intended to hold handbags. A moss garden separates a suite's capacious bedroom from the sitting room. The Water's Edge spa features an infinity pool engineered to maintain stillness even as the building moves, while windows allow views of the city from 85 floors up.*

VOA
Associates
Incorporated

MARRIOTT BEIJING NORTHEAST, CHINA

China's Hainan Island, on the same latitude as Hawaii, lures tourists with sandy beaches, waters fit for scuba diving, and lush tropical rainforests. Far north of it is the Marriott Beijing Northeast, in the hustle and bustle near the Forbidden City's Imperial Palace. Aiming to bring the experience of "China's Hawaii" to Beijing visitors, the firm—known throughout Asia as VOA Architecture Design—dreamed up a dramatic lobby that includes a large water feature, towering palm trees, the sounds of tropical waterfalls, and the unique aromas of the Chinese rainforest. The high-vaulted glass ceiling is LED backlit to create a luminous, ever-changing blue "sky." The island-oasis theme is echoed elsewhere as well: A water curtain divides the main lounge into two zones, the Quan Spa focuses on hydrotherapy, and the suites' baths are visible from the bedrooms. Nosh on Cantonese and Sichuan fish dishes in one of three restaurants, Choy's Seafood, or enjoy the Dream spa treatment, a deep-sea submersion with pure marine elements. You can't really scuba dive in the 25-meter indoor lap pool. But you can sit in the hot tub, take a deep breath, and be transported nonetheless.

Clockwise from top:
The doors to the executive lounge, which features a boardroom, spacious work areas, and panoramic views of Beijing. A traditional tea bar gets a modern face, with sleek furnishings and a neutral palette accented with red. The ceiling of the lobby atrium, with an LED-backlit vaulted glass ceiling whose color shifts throughout the day to mimic the sky above. ➤

"In the context of Beijing's hectic central business district,
the hotel—with its emphasis on nature—is a welcoming oasis"

—RICHARD FAWELL

Clockwise from top:
The spa entryway
uses organic shapes
and a natural palette.
The entrance and
bar of the Chinese
restaurant overlooks
the lobby's sculptural
glass pendant,
reminiscent of
undersea bubbles.
The swimming pool
and hot tub provide
relaxation along with
downtown views. ➣

1 ENTRY
2 RECEPTION
3 RETAIL
4 BAKERY/COFFEE
5 WATER FEATURE
6 WINE BAR
7 TEA BAR

0   10   20   40

1 EXECUTIVE OFFICES
2 ATRIUM
3 MEETING ROOM
4 PRIVATE OFFICES

400 guest rooms
9,000 sf (ballroom)
30,000 sf (meeting area)

PROJECT TEAM RICHARD FAWELL, PATRICIA ROTONDO, NAN ZHOU, CHRISTOPHER GROESBECK,
KRIS YOKOO, SERENA YU WEN, JEANNINE NORMAN, JULIE ZENG

PHOTOGRAPHY FU XING

www.voa.com

Clockwise from opposite top: The cobalt-accented residential suite features a view of the master bath from the bedroom area, as well as a living room and electric fireplace. A tilework spiral marks the entrance to the massage spa. Light walls in the elevator lobby of the conference center contrast with the dark floors and ceiling. The breakout space in the conference center, where some hotel staff work in the open. The hotel's fitness area, with dark-wood finishes, ample natural and artificial lighting, and a wave-like ceiling design.

Wilson Associates

GRAND HYATT SHENZHEN HOTEL, CHINA

Guests arriving at this soaring property are directed to a sky lobby on the 33rd floor. Above that, five spectacularly illuminated levels of amenities give the building crown the look of a stylized Chinese lantern—thanks in part to contributions from the Singapore-based interiors team long before construction began. They carved out impressive multistory spaces, creating vantages and sight lines to allow views between floors—and to the lush green mountains in the distance.

The Show Kitchen, one of eight eateries, features dramatically tall ceilings that "heighten" the dining experience. China Lodge has 14 private dining rooms rendered in dark tones and accented with slate stonework. The VIP dining room is approached via a stone-clad Zen garden complete with reflecting pool. The Belle-Vue, a classic European restaurant, presents a series of "live"

cooking pods, with chefs' preparing food practically tableside; its glass-wrapped private dining room is filled with rustic liquor barrels.

Closer to the ground, the Shui Xiang spa offers holistic treatment rooms overlooking the podium roof garden. In the shaft of the tower, floor-to-ceiling windows offer views of the bustling city of 15 million, or neighboring Hong Kong, across the border. Guest accommodations are generous, with bathrooms nearly as large as sleeping areas. They feature a wet room that contains a spacious rain shower and freestanding tub—the entirety of which can be handily screened for privacy via sliding fretwork panels fitted with glass that fogs at the touch of a button.

491 guest rooms

Clockwise from opposite top: In the sky lobby, reception is framed by lantern-inspired lighting. A freestanding tub in the Grand King bathroom. Sliding fretwork panels integrate with electronically activated privacy-glass panels. Despite its 40-foot ceiling, the penthouse living area has a residential feel courtesy of a fireplace that divides the space. The penthouse whiskey cellar contrasts wooden barrels with elegant shaded chandeliers and sleek glass walls. The balcony penthouse living area overlooks six floors of food and beverage destinations. The mezzanine lounge.

PROJECT TEAM CEDRIC JACCARD, JOANNE YONG, DAN KWAN, REDEN LANTICAN, MILDRED BERMUDEZ, JANICE JACOB, THOMAS LEE, CONNIE GLAZER, RACHEL TAN

PHOTOGRAPHY CHRISTOPHER CYPERT

www.wilsonassociates.com

197,000 sf
150 guest rooms
and suites

SFA Design

HILTON WINDHOEK PLAZA HOTEL, NAMIBIA

Namibia's capital and one of the fastest-growing tourist destinations in Southern Africa, Windhoek has a posh downtown that stands in stark contrast to the wildlife reserves, conservation parks, and vast Namib desert just beyond its borders. Conceived as a connecting point between those two worlds, the city's first five-star hotel is a full-on luxury property, which pays tribute to its setting via locally sourced elements and stylized riffs on safari chic.

Materials crafted by indigenous artisans lend an authentic touch, as do the abundance of furnishings specified in Africa. Wood, stone, and tile from the region were utilized for floor and wall coverings. In guest quarters, backlit acrylic panels flanking the fabric-covered headboards depict the sea, sky, and sand. Water—a cherished resource in this oasis—is a recurring theme, expressed in abundant reflective finishes. Carved-glass tabletops add sparkle to the lobby lounge. Glass pendant lights rain down from the soaring two-story atrium, where a glazed wall mural depicts an abstract desert landscape. And in lieu of solid walls, translucent panels divide guest quarters. The best place to contemplate nature's collision with the manmade is on the roof, where a plein air pool and bar await.

Clockwise from top: In the atrium, dangling molded-glass raindrops establish the water motif. The lobby's brown and turquoise palette was inspired by sand and sea, while zebra-print accessories allude to the region's wildlife. Backpainted-glass panels enclose a closet in a guest-room foyer. ➤

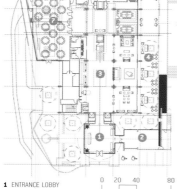

1 ENTRANCE LOBBY

2 COFFEE SHOP

3 RECEPTION AND WAITING AREA

4 TERRACE

5 MEETING ROOM

6 BUSINESS CENTER

7 CONFERENCE AREA

Clockwise from top:
The rooftop Sky bar's extralong couches afford stunning views. In the Kalabar restaurant and bar, an illuminated acrylic panel celebrates native plants; leather tub chairs from a South African supplier lend a clubby vibe. A bath's stone floor is inset with river-rock mosaics; a free-standing tub with Hansgrohe fixtures provides a sultry soak. The mural wall in a superior suite. Glass panels divide a guest room's sleeping and bathing areas.

PROJECT TEAM KARA SMITH, ROSIE FEINBERG

ARCHITECT OF RECORD WASSERFALL MUNTING ARCHITECTS

PHOTOGRAPHY DOOK ROSS

www.sfadesign.com

237,000 sf (overall)
7,150 sf (meeting/event space)
218 guest rooms and suites

Peter Silling & Associates

JUMEIRAH FRANKFURT HOTEL, GERMANY

In determining a design direction for this towering addition to the Frankfurt skyline, the firm had to look beyond the hotel itself. The building would be one of four in an innovative new development whose centerpiece is the Thurn und Taxis Palais, a reconstruction of an 18th-century structure damaged in World War II. How would an unabashedly contemporary hotel measure up beside a baroque palace with an illustrious pedigree?

Quite well, it turns out. Public spaces and amenities are a study in luxurious subtlety, with an emphasis on richly figured wood and marble finishes. Business travelers and event planners have stately (and copious) facilities to avail themselves of, while foodies can head to one of three destinations. Just off reception is the Ember Lounge & Bar, where dark hues are offset by saffron accents. At Max on One, by edgy Japanese design firm Super Potato, guests can choose from a menu of not only inventive German/Austrian fare but also dining environments—from a relaxed lounge to a chef's table in the kitchen proper. In the bistro, Le Petit Palais, marble floors and tabletops offset ocher slipper chairs and a sleek banquette; an undulating ceiling and patterned walls envelop the space in warm and spicy tones.

The Jumeirah features the largest guest rooms in Frankfurt (377 square feet at the least), with stunning city and palace vistas. Minimalist but never sparse, they're smartly configured to look even bigger: In many quarters, the bath opens directly onto the living area and furnishings float in the center of floor for an airier feel. Palettes are subdued and soothing; original canvases by Leipzig artist Hartwig Ebersbach add bold color—and ensure each room is unique.

From left: Named for its open fireplace, the Ember Lounge & Bar is a low-key spot overlooking the Thurn und Taxis Palais. Textures abound in Le Petit Palais: Cool marble flooring with mosaic trim underscores a wavelike wood-veneer ceiling treatment, similarly woody book-matched walls, and furnishings in caramel and chocolate. ➘

1 ENTRY

2 EMBER LOUNGE & BAR

3 RECEPTION

4 ELEVATOR LOBBY

5 WAITING AREA

6 LE PETIT PALAIS

ARCHITECT OF RECORD KSP ENGEL UND ZIMMERMANN
PHOTOGRAPHY COURTESY OF JUMEIRAH FRANKFURT HOTEL AND
PETER SILLING & ASSOCIATES

hotelinteriordesign.de

Clockwise from opposite: *A padded headboard wall and silk area rug mark a Skyline deluxe room; a desk between the sleeping and living zones anchors a swiveling flatscreen TV that's viewable from both spaces. Meetings take place under an imposing crystal chandelier. The window above a deluxe room's headboard offers a view into the streamlined open bathroom. Each room features an original painting by Hartwig Ebersbach and a built-in desk inspired by a portable antique secretary.*

VOA
Associates
Incorporated

RENAISSANCE SHANGHAI
PUTUO HOTEL, CHINA

The elements of wind and water have long played an essential role in this port city's success, and they still do. By dint of its location—on the Huangpu river, in eastern China—Shanghai was destined to be a hub of industry and commerce. Once junks plied the waters; today it's cargo ships, as the city is the world's busiest container port and a global financial center.

In tackling the interiors of this new hotel, completed just in time for Shanghai to host the 2010 World Expo, the firm (known in Asia as VOA Architecture Design) settled on a maritime theme. Principal designer Richard Fawell had in mind the swirling winds and waters that first—and literally—brought foreign travelers and trade to these shores.

Curvaceous shapes—circles, arcs, spirals—and grand lighting (often in combination) are cornerstones of the design, and this is apparent upon first sight. Guests are swept into reception on a marble floor of churning waves, which is carried out in subtly gradated neutral shades.

The hotel has three restaurants to explore: the Japanese grill restaurant Yuzu, the traditional New Dynasty, and Café BLD, an all-day buffet featuring an open kitchen and an outdoor garden with private patio. And business visitors will find themselves well provided for. Support services are copious, as are the options in accommodations, among them meeting rooms, a boardroom, a function room, and a grand ballroom.

11,076 sf (meeting rooms)
60,480 sf (grand ballroom)

353 guest rooms and
13 suites

24-hour fitness center, atrium, media room, and business center

Clockwise from top: The hotel entrance remains roomy thanks to the grand stairway, whose glass treads and banisters are paired with polished chrome railings. At the tea bar, grouped tubular pendants dangle above a maître d' station faced with overlapping strips of light. A marble pattern eddies on the floor before the curved reception desk, as a sculptural chandelier— suggesting swirling water or an unfurling rose— hovers overhead. ➤

"Details mimic the swirling character of water spouts, a motif inspired by Shanghai's long-standing maritime connection with the West"—RICHARD FAWELL

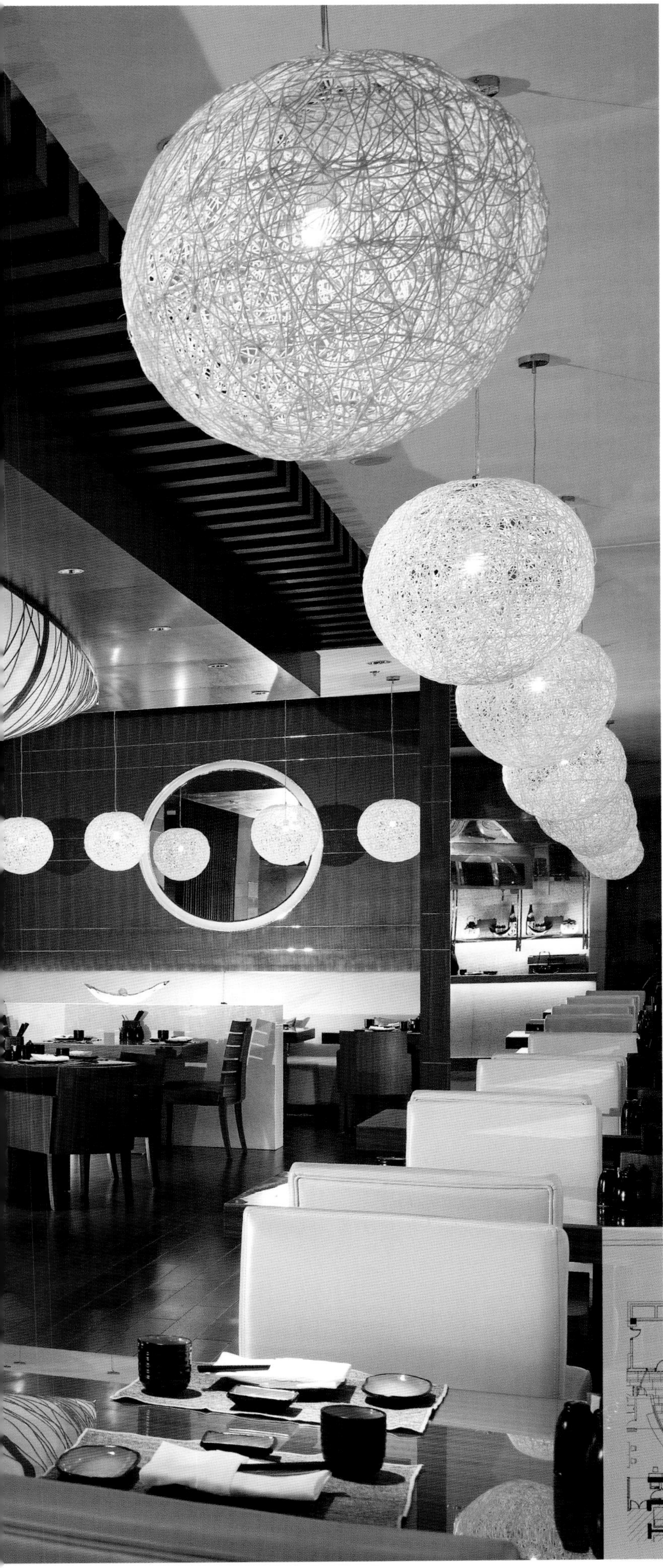

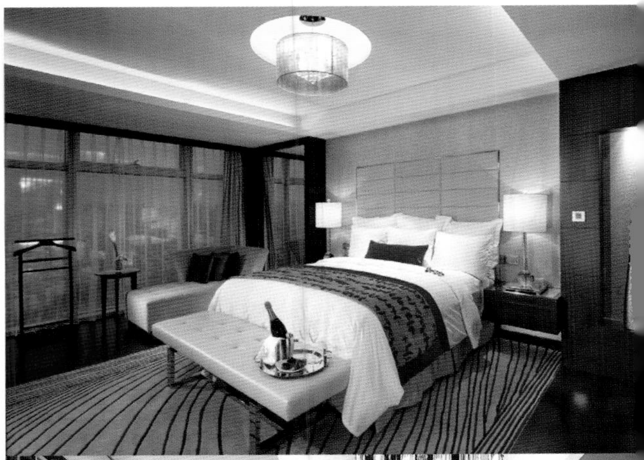

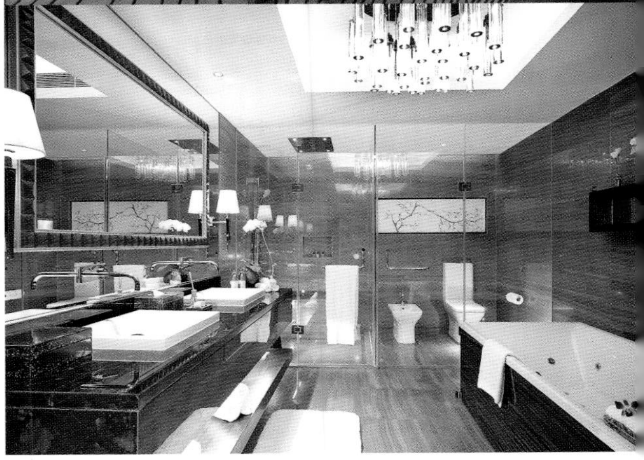

Clockwise from left:
In Yuzu, the Japanese grill, a hull-shaped light fixture dominates, accentuating the room's length; a porthole mirror on the rear partition continues the nautical motif. A comfortable executive suite bedroom offers sweeping skyline views. Clad entirely in marble, the open bathroom in the same suite features a whirlpool bath, double sinks, and a recessed chandelier.

1 RECEPTION
2 CONCIERGE
3 WATER ELEMENT
4 BUSINESS CENTER
5 BAR
6 MEDIA ROOM

0 10 20 40

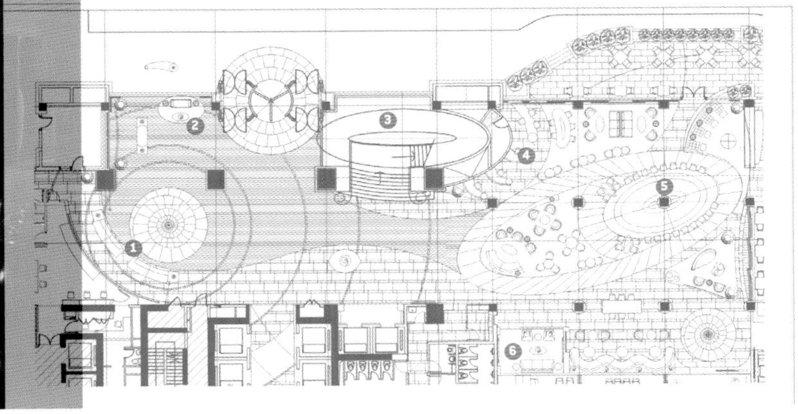

PROJECT TEAM RICHARD FAWELL, PATRICIA ROTONDO, NAN ZHOU, CHRISTOPHER GROESBECK, KRIS YOKOO, SERENA YU WEN, JEANNINE NORMAN, JULIE ZENG

PHOTOGRAPHY FU XING

www.voa.com

Clockwise from top left: The spa counter's glowing backdrop radiates warmth at check-in. Cozy seating under a high-drama chandelier in the great room's lobby. In the traditional Chinese restaurant, New Dynasty, fretwork panels create intimate spaces without sacrificing light. The lounge bar's "tornado" crystal chandelier. New Dynasty's private VIP room can accommodate business meetings and small family gatherings. Guests swim laps in or unwind beside an inviting 25-meter pool. The long view to the lobby elevator.

HBA

HOTEL INDIGO SHANGHAI ON THE BUND, CHINA

180 guest rooms

Clockwise from top:
The view from the
mural to a lounge area
overlooking the Bund;
plants grow amid the
panes of the latter's
"live" glass wall. The
wavelike feature in
the lobby is the first
of many touches
referencing water
and nautical activity.
The Quay library,
which focuses on
area history. ➤

Many hospitality projects seek to blend tradition and modernity, but this riverfront hotel on the Bund succeeds better than most. Perhaps it's because connecting guests to surrounding communities is key to the brand's philosophy— or perhaps because the port city has such a storied past to draw upon, evolving as it has from shipping and trade center to international player.

Either way, the results are soon evident. Ultramodernity reigns in the lobby and registration area, where undulating walls of grooved plywood snake up at floor level to form the check-in desk. On the desk's arrival side, vibrant turquoise Swan chairs await (Why this isn't standard practice? one suddenly wonders), and in a pleasingly symmetrical design gesture, squares recessed in the ceiling echo the hue.

On the opposite side of the lobby wall stretches a handpainted mural of a Bund street scene, a realist rendering that borrowed from vintage photographs taken nearby. Businessmen, students, and tourists share busy sidewalks before a pagoda-style structure with a canopied ground floor and fretwork balconies.

Common spaces and guest quarters integrate eras. In the café, cube armchairs and minimalist tables dovetail with an artfully arrayed display of rustic cookware. A subdued suite gets a jolt from cheery pillows, a bold round rug, and a boudoir-ish pink table lamp...to say nothing of the striking Pudong skyline—Huangpu river view on two sides.

PROJECT TEAM ANDREW MOORE, JULIAN COOMBS, LIAN MIEW CHING, VIN LEONG KOK WAI, DAISY YANG
ARCHITECTURE FIRM GENSLER, SHANGHAI
PHOTOGRAPHY KEN HAYDEN PHOTOGRAPHY (1, 2, 4, 6), JIMMY COHRSSEN (3, 5)
www.hbadesign.com

Clockwise from left:
Strong elemental materials were used throughout, such as the marble, steel, and wood that characterize the winetasting area of the restaurant. The guest suite's canopy bed is a modern homage to the traditional Chinese wedding bed. Drinks are served at a backlit onyx counter at Char Bar & Grill on the top floor. In the Me Space, part of the Quay lounge/ sanctuary, birdcage-like nooks offer up river views.

1 ELEVATOR LOBBY
2 MEETING ROOMS
3 BUSINESS LOUNGE
4 ME SPACE
5 FOOT MASSAGE
6 DINING AREA
7 BAR

0   10   20   40

FOUR SEASONS HOTEL LONDON AT PARK LANE

Pierre-Yves Rochon

In 1970, Four Seasons founder Isadore Sharpe debuted his inventive Inn on the Park in London. Among its cutting-edge miracles were one-hour pressing and guest rooms with multiple phones. To move that property, now called Four Seasons Hotel London at Park Lane, from '70s modern to '30s moderne, Pierre-Yves Rochon supervised 28 months of refurbishment.

The gut renovation is Deco-inspired but avoids period clichés thanks to overscale elements and an eclectic mix of furnishings. The double-height tea salon features a huge antique chandelier and retro hand-molded plaster wall reliefs of leaping deer, plus devilish bright red Arne Jacobsen Egg chairs and a matching crimson-lacquered Kawai grand piano.

Clockwise from top: A guest room with a bay window overlooking Green Park. Crisp white finishes combine with a bold brocade wall covering in the early-arrival lounge. Amaranto restaurant's main dining room has a fabric-wrapped ceiling and marble floors. ➤

Set into the salon's gallery wall are vitrines showcasing glass objects in a spectrum of colors. An ethereal lounge welcomes early arrivals with white-marble-top Saarinen pedestal tables and an azure brocade accent wall under a ceiling mural of clouds in the sky. Once in their rooms, guests find views of Green Park framed by decor featuring either "brunette" tones, for rooms accented with mahogany, or "blonde"—think figured sycamore offset with bronze mirror, polished chrome, and bed linens sporting outsize plaids. Consider that tradition tweaked, old chap.

1 FRONT DESK

2 LOBBY

3 TEA SALON

4 GALLERY

5 BAR/LOUNGE

6 RESTAURANT

Clockwise from opposite top:
A gallery showcases rainbow-color glass. Champagne and cream tones prevail in the Asian-inspired garden suite. The lounge area of Amaranto restaurant has full-height chrome-and-glass wine displays and tufted-fabric walls. The garden-suite bedroom's sienna and butter-yellow tones reiterate the palette of the hotel's public areas. The lobby tea salon features hand-molded bas-reliefs and mirror panels that create the illusion of a much bigger portal.

0 10 20   40

PROJECT TEAM PIERRE-YVES ROCHON, ANNICK ROCHON, JEAN-MARIE HEIDERSCHEID, JENNY JOHNSON, LAURIE ALLEN, PHILIPPE JOUANNEAULT, LARA LESKAJ

ARCHITECT OF RECORD REARDON SMITH ARCHITECTS

PHOTOGRAPHY RICHARD WAITE (1, 2, 4, 8), PETER VITALE (5, 7), ANTHONY PARKINSON (3, 6)

www.pyr-design.com

Bilkey Llinas Design

FOUR SEASONS HANGZHOU, CHINA

89 keys

Restaurant, music bar, meeting rooms, ballroom, young adult center, and retail

Clockwise from right: Woven-silk triptychs, positioned over headboards, adorn sumptuous guest bedrooms. The designer's plush, delicately hued upholstery befits a Sung Dynasty villa; the woodsy palette was chosen to harmonize with the fretwork windows. In the lobby atrium, a black stone infinity fountain burbles beneath a spiraling custom chandelier. At twilight, a reflecting pool mirrors tile pagoda roofs.

"In heaven there is paradise," say the Chinese, "on Earth there is Hangzhou." Fresh from the Silk Road, Marco Polo proclaimed the place splendid. Today the waters of the city's central West Lake—ringed since antiquity with temples and picturesque pagodas—also lap at the shores of this resort's nine lush, manicured acres.

Surprisingly, the entire complex is new. Presented with these buildings of whitewashed stucco and gray clay roof tiles, both signatures of classical Sung Dynasty villas, the Hong Kong–based designers sought to make spaces that were deeply Chinese but not overpoweringly so.

The 78 guest rooms, assorted suites, and three villas have refreshingly simple contemporary interiors with traditional wooden fretwork in the windows; inlaid marble flooring echoes the motifs. The typically monochrome Sung palette—white and gray, plus natural wood tones—was warmed with beige, soft yellow, and a smidgen of black.

In the lobby, a crystal chandelier symbolizing happiness and long life spirals above a gentle central fountain; the light the fixture casts bounces off the water's shimmering surface and returns, ripple-like, to the ceiling.

A 4,000-square-foot ballroom, able to accommodate sizable banquet meetings, features crystal chandeliers and rich silk-upholstered walls. And as the region is famed for its silks, the designers commissioned tapestries—woven locally, with images from nature—to hang in the lobby and above guest-room beds.

PROJECT TEAM ROBERT BILKEY, OSCAR LLINAS, XIN OUYANG, JENNY TING, ROCIO SAENZ, RAVI YEE

ARCHITECT OF RECORD ZHEJIANG GREENTOWN ORIENTAL ARCHITECTURE DESIGN

PHOTOGRAPHY KEN SEET

www.bilkeyllinas.com

540 sf (guest rooms)

ISSI Design

@GALLERY SUITES HOTEL, SHANGHAI, CHINA

Clockwise from above: A retro bank lamp illuminates the desk area of an Art Deco grand suite. Shikumen-style brickwork clads a guest-room bath, which has a glass-enclosed loo and walk-in shower. Silk-covered screens wrap the living area, which is outfitted in a mix of vintage pieces and Deco-inspired custom furnishings. In lieu of headboards, beds are framed by contemporary artwork. A guest-room rendering.

Catering to creative-minded jet-setters, this boutique hotel has a multicultural past. The 1933 Art Deco building, in the French Concession, was once the home of a Russian princess. Its adaptive reuse re-creates period glamour by grafting traditional touches onto modern construction.

The structure posed a few challenges, namely an abundance of load-bearing walls that couldn't be demolished. So the designers worked around them, transforming blockages into feature walls that divvy the interiors into more intimate confines. To conserve square footage, living and sleeping areas are separated by a floor-to-ceiling TV cabinet that swivels to service both spaces. Bathrooms, meanwhile, are demarcated by sliding panels and open fretwork screens rather than solid walls; the water closet and shower are tucked behind glass. Walls are brick, a feature common to Shikumen townhouses nearby.

Finishes and accessories reinforce the historic vibe. Lending a fashion-forward touch are wall panels covered in the same type of silk brocade used to make cheongsams. Old-school table fans lend a nostalgic feel. And sensuous color photographs by up-and-coming artists instill an air of modern exoticism, in a happy collision of old and new.

PROJECT TEAM ANDY LEUNG, RAY LEE, QIAN FENG
PHOTOGRAPHY HYPHOTO
www.issi-design.com

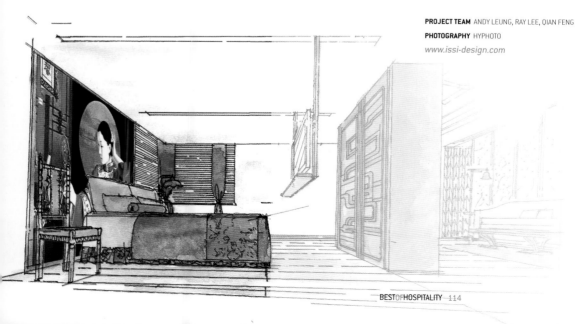

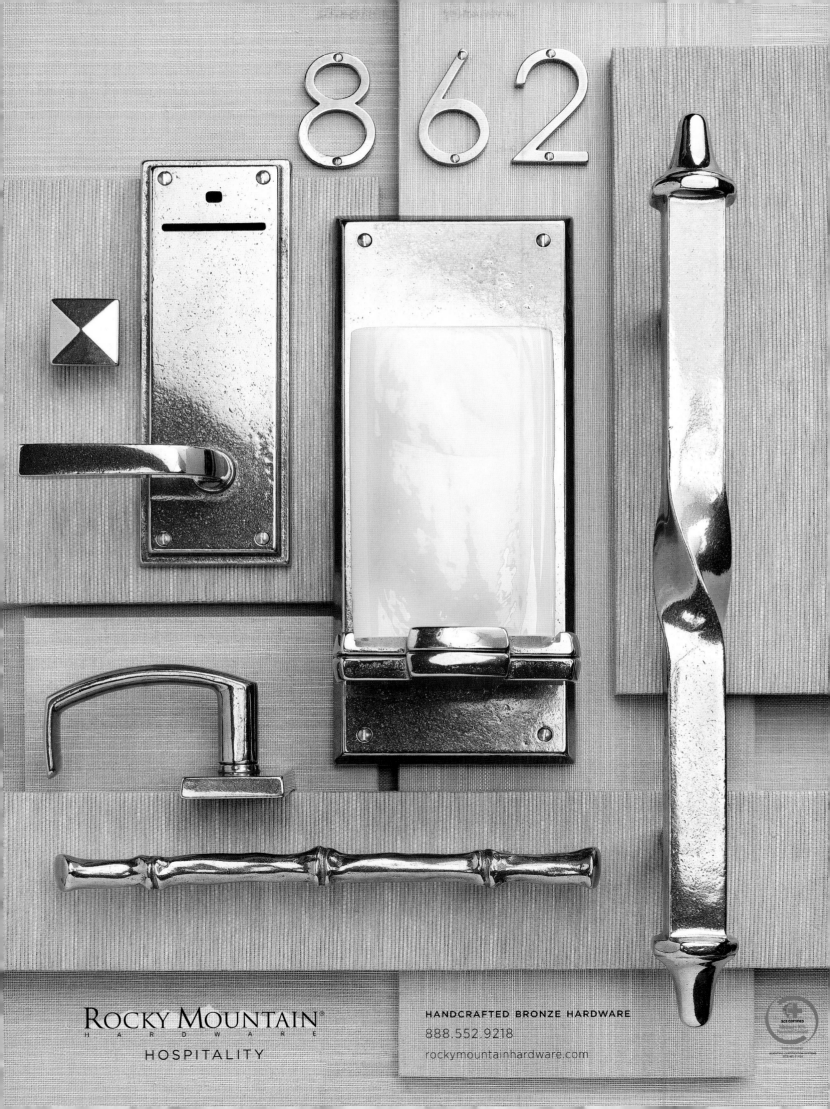

resort hotel

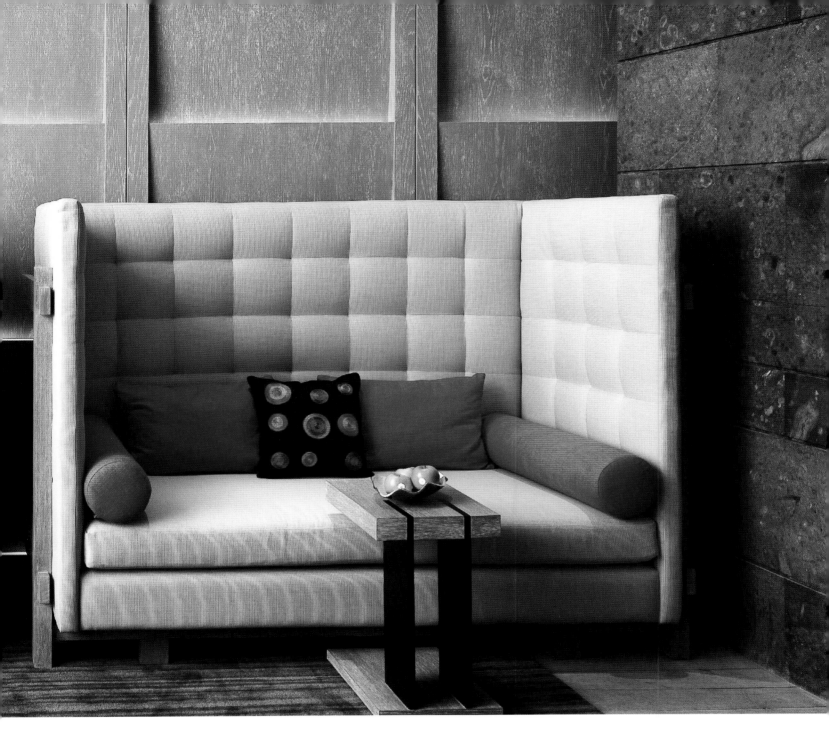

It's always smart to start with what you have. Especially when those assets include a drop-dead setting: a tree-topped mountain, a steep cliff overlooking a crystal-clear bay, or—in the case of a certain luxury cruise ship—an unending cerulean sea.

At resort properties, the landscape invariably sparks myriad design details—from lobby finishes and guest-room furnishings to floral-print upholstery and saturated palettes—which then serve to coax the outdoors in. The use of regional materials and indigenous craftspeople and techniques becomes a kind of shorthand to convey a local sensibility. Take One Steamboat Place's sculptural lighting fixtures, the Royal Hawaiian's *kapa mua* quilts, or the Ritz-Carlton Lake Tahoe's collection of works by nearby artists. Although earthiness prevails, so does fantasy, as designers dream up bravado gestures to transport guests to faraway—and sometimes mythical—lands (Bali, the Seychelles, Atlantis). *Looks like it's time to go native.*

AB Concept

W RETREAT & SPA BALI—SEMINYAK INDONESIA

This beachfront property's evocative decor plays against type: The project brief was to upend expectations of Balinese resort style. To firm codirectors Ed Ng and Terence Ngan, that meant respecting the island's cultural heritage—and referencing its distinct natural features—while giving traditional Indonesian motifs a bold, contemporary twist. Thus a recurrence of neon-pink hues sparked by Balinese sunsets, cheeky landscape references, and sly abstractions of vernacular architecture—from pagodalike pendant lights to stepped ceilings recalling the silhouettes of local temples.

The paisley design on the lobby ceiling honors Hindu henna-work, blowing it up to grand proportions; below, terrazzo flooring shimmering with inlaid shells was cut in sinuous curves to resemble leaves. The wall behind reception is actually a mirrored timber screen supporting handblown-glass jars, each housing a capiz shell that emits a singsongy whistle when it vibrates in the sea breeze. While this open structure encourages natural ventilation during the dry season, monsoon shutters ensure full protection during the wet months.

Speaking of the elements, guest suites bring the outdoors in. Sleeping areas showcase restful shades of green, like those of the island's lush jungles. Carpeting mimics lotus ponds. And skylights above soaking tubs feature fretwork that casts dappling shadows similar to water reflections. Seems that at least one Bali-resort trope was preserved...the otherworldly sense of tranquility.

Clockwise from above: A terrace off the lobby is lined with generous daybeds. A curved feature wall treated to piano-finish black lacquer forms a dramatic display in W The Store, lit by an acrylic chandelier. In the EWOW Suite's private spa, massage tables look onto the Indian Ocean and, through an oculus, the azure sky. ➤

333,681 sf
158 retreats and suites and 79 pool villas
The two-bedroom EWOW Suite boasts
a living room, dining room, show kitchen,
en suite spa, study, and balcony with
wraparound ocean views

Above the wind-chime screen is the henna-inspired design, hand-painted by a local artisan. The nest sculpture was purchased from a store nearby.

PROJECT TEAM ED NG, TERENCE NGAN

PHOTOGRAPHY CHESTER ONG

www.abconcept.net

1 ENTRY

2 BATHROOM

3 SLEEPING AREA

4 LIVING AREA

5 BALCONY

Clockwise from top: Guest retreats feature weathered-oak headboards and throws detailed with hand-stitched leaves. Furnishings in the W lounge were crafted with natural materials, including local timber and volcanic stone. In the two-bedroom villa, the sculptural seating was designed to resemble flower petals. Each of the 79 villas has its own pool.

"Throughout, we fused festive colors and distinctive architectural shapes to instill an adventurous spirit"
—ED NG

72 guest rooms
Lobby bar and breakfast lounge

Jiun Ho

HOTEL RENEW, OAHU, HAWAII

Every project faces challenges, but Jiun Ho faced two especially daunting ones in completely redesigning this property on Oahu: the building and the location. Fortunately the client, a real estate investor with no hotel experience, was amenable and allowed the firm (nearly) carte blanche on the creative side.

Built as an apartment complex, the structure was never intended to meet the demands of hospitality design; the firm had to work within the existing space. One of the project's finest features—its site on a breathtaking small island—had drawbacks, too. Though half the interior boasted ocean views, the scarcity of materials meant that everything had to be ordered and shipped from the mainland.

The spa hotel departs from the typical Hawaiian getaway awash in tropical trappings. Ho's design is modern and tranquil, a place for guests to retreat and recharge. A monochrome scheme was carried out in furniture, lighting, wall coverings, and even employee uniforms. The surroundings supplied many details: a wave motif on headboards, linens, wallpaper, and floors; artwork and light fixtures made with seashells; shoji screens, reflecting the area's strong Asian influence, as window treatments. Ho himself designed almost every element of the decor—from linens and lighting to café tables and guest-room desks.

In overcoming space limitations, the firm designed guest storage allowing luggage and personal items to be hidden from sight—supporting the spare aesthetic so conducive to the successful spa experience.

Clockwise from above: A feature wall behind the entry desk is clad in a mosaic of river rocks. The rejuvenated hotel facade. River rocks also surround a water feature in the elevator lobby, brightened by fabric pendants; sheers veil the snug sitting area from heat but not light. ➤

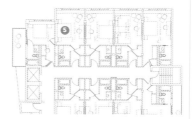

PHOTOGRAPHY DAVID DUNCAN LIVINGSTON
www.jiunho.com

0 10 20   40

1 LOBBY SEATING AREA

2 RECEPTION

3 ELEVATOR LOBBY

4 LOBBY BAR

5 GUEST ROOM

Clockwise from opposite: In a guest room, an Eames Aluminum Group chair services the glass-top custom desk. Corian café tables furnish the lobby bar. A guest-room dressing station's mirror doubles as a light fixture. Dark-stained wood wall treatments with a wave detail lend a restful touch to sleeping quarters. Ho designed most pieces in the hotel, including this furniture in the lobby sitting area.

1,539 guest rooms
Grand lobby, aquarium, 6 restaurants, bar, spa, and lounge

ATLANTIS, THE PALM, DUBAI

Wilson Associates

The Dallas-based interiors team coordinated more than 30 international consultants and flew upwards of a half-million miles over the course of six years to realize this resort fantasia in the United Arab Emirates. The massive structure serves as the focal point of Dubai's Palm Jumeirah island, an improbable manmade sandbar.

Extravagant gestures abound, including the 30-foot Dale Chihuly crystal column that seems to erupt volcanically beneath the lobby's sea urchin–inspired dome. Eight sculptural fish columns ring the structure, while murals painted by Spanish artist Albino Gonzalez depict the mythical ancient city for which the property is named. ShuiQi, the 20,000-square-foot spa and fitness center, features whimsical sea horse–shape door handles, fish-theme fountains, relief walls portraying sea kelp, and treatment rooms with vaulted lava-stone ceilings.

The large public gathering area called Poseidon's Court is furnished with a golden throne fit for a sea god, natch. One wall has a double-height acrylic window revealing the imagined wreckage of a lost city submerged in Ambassador Lagoon. This 2.8 million–gallon marine habitat contains 65,000 aquatic animals. A seafood restaurant, as well as the master bedrooms of two suites, overlooks the lagoon through floor-to-ceiling acrylic windows—all for the illusion of undersea living.

Not hooked on fish? Among the food and beverage options are a traditional Arabic coffeehouse, a caravan-inspired restaurant, and a steakhouse featuring a custom wine room stocked with some 3,000 bottles.

Clockwise from top: The master bedroom of the Lost Chamber suite features a fish-eye's view of the Ambassador Lagoon through an acrylic window. A rain shower cascades into the spa treatment pool, ringed by antiqued-bronze "seaweed" metalwork. The lobby's sea urchin dome crowns a Dale Chihuly sculpture. The 27 spa treatment rooms are accessed via bridges spanning running water. The 33-foot-deep Poseidon Court showcases remnants of a mythical Atlantis. The dining room of the presidential suite sports handpainted ceiling murals and bespoke area rugs depicting sea life.

PROJECT TEAM JAMES CARRY, MAY POON, CRISTIAN VIDAURE, YOOSOOK LEE, PAUL ADAMS, RALF SEBECKE, ANN HSIEH, KAREN FILIPSKI, LIZA SETIAWAN, SARITA STEWART, SHELLEY THOMSON, THERESA HELGREN, ANDREA CEPALEE
PHOTOGRAPHY COURTESY OF ATLANTIS, THE PALM
www.wilsonassociates.com

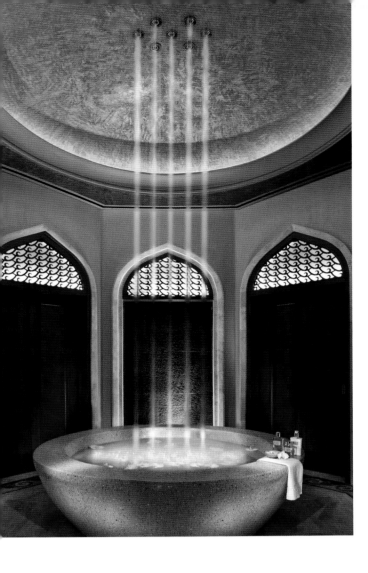

Philpotts Interiors

THE ROYAL HAWAIIAN, A LUXURY
COLLECTION RESORT, WAIKIKI

Coprincipals Marion Philpotts-Miller and Lowell Tom faced
numerous challenges in updating this 1927 landmark hotel.
Given an aggressive timeline and modest furniture budget,
they were tasked with executing a historic restoration that
would appeal to a diverse clientele—from modern-minded
jet-setters to mainland vacationers inclined to romanticize
Hawaiian style—while also pleasing local preservationists
and nostalgists.

One defining feature met those needs and unified the
public and private areas. The hotel's signature fuchsia was
maintained but applied in unexpected ways—brightening
elements such as wall coverings, painted ceilings, carpet
patterns, and upholstery fabrics. Likewise balancing old
and new is the refurbished koa woodwork, including
baseboards, trims, and the front desk (the latter was
reworked to accommodate current technology). Classic
Moorish-style side tables were freshened up with shiny
lacquer, and old but structurally unsound coconut trees
dotting the property were salvaged and handcrafted
into Hawaiian *pahu* drums.

Another hurdle was standardizing 350 guest rooms,
each with a unique layout. Decorative elements were
chosen to make cramped rooms feel more spacious
and large rooms more intimate. Clever placement of art,
lighting, and furniture helps patrons navigate a maze of
honeycomb-terracotta-brick walls.

A testament to the redesign's success? Guests are
already inquiring about purchasing replicas of the
hotel's furnishings for their own abodes.

Clockwise from right:
A restored painted-wood ceiling and freshly whitewashed walls distinguish a sitting area off the lobby, outfitted with a mix of new and rehabbed vintage furniture. A custom kapa mua quilt covers a bed in the King Kamehameha Suite. The hotel's original pink-tinted Moorish-style facade was returned to its former glory. An elevator lobby's wall covering, upholstery, and carpets in the hotel's trademark color. The check-in desk and surrounding millwork was built from native koa, which has a distinctive red grain; the settee is an antique from India.

333,681 sf
Philpotts Interiors renovated 350 of the
528 historical guest rooms and suites
Luxury spa, pool, 20 specialty boutiques,
4 restaurants, a business center, and
banquet and meeting facilities

PROJECT TEAM LYNN ARRIOLA, ANNE TANAKA, KRISTIE KIGGINS, DAWN CHING,
RON UYESUGI, ZOA ZACK, MICHELLE JAIME
ARCHITECT OF RECORD WCIT ARCHITECTURE
PHOTOGRAPHY ART GRAY

www.philpotts.net

GRAND-HÔTEL DU CAP-FERRAT, FRANCE

Pierre-Yves Rochon

Perched on a peninsula in the Côte d'Azur, a short distance from Monaco, this well-heeled resort has operated since the early 20th century (save for a few pauses during World Wars). In enlisting PYR to execute a redesign, the client requested an all-white interior, which the firm interpreted as an airy mélange of pale wood and stone brightened with hints of celadon and seafoam.

The original oceanfront rotunda lounge, designed by Gustave Eiffel, offers a series of voluptuous couches in a serene room accented by gilded mirrors positioned to reflect the seaside light. The nearby bar and restaurant evoke the property's gardens via organic patterns and prints that bedeck the mosaic floors, carpets, upholstery, and even tableware. For an extra level of relaxation (not to mention pampering), there's the spa, reached by a sinuous ramp punctuated with wood sculptures and dramatically washed by recessed lights.

The design team reconfigured guest rooms to be more spacious and added a new wing for suites, graced with floor-to-ceiling windows overlooking a terrace and private infinity pool. The aqueous palette continues into the living areas, accented with paintings and sculptures by French artists—who all happen to be frequent hotel visitors.

Clockwise from above: Marble walls envelop a guest bathroom. Lalique birds alight on a lantern near the entry; the same crystal forms the table base. In the rotunda lounge, celadon lamps accent seating upholstered in creamy linen and silk. A wood sculpture points the way to the spa, accessed via a winding ramp. ➤

1 ENTRY HALL
2 RECEPTION
3 BAR
4 INTERIOR GARDEN
5 SALON
6 TERRACE
7 JEWELRY SHOP
8 GUEST ROOM

0 10 20 40

PROJECT TEAM PIERRE-YVES ROCHON, ANNICK ROCHON, JEAN-MARIE HEIDERSCHEID, STÉPHANE RENAUD, HERVE JAILLET
ARCHITECTS OF RECORD EXTENSION: LUC SVETCHI. EXISTING BUILDING: MICHAEL ZANDER
PHOTOGRAPHY CHRISTIAN SARRAMON

www.pyr-design.com

Clockwise from above: The rotunda lounge looks out at the Mediterranean through oversize windows framed by silk drapes. A canopy bed in the guest quarters creates a cosseting room within a room. The spa staircase's wave-like balustrade is skimmed in Venetian plaster. A sculpture carved from a salvaged tree trunk anchors the spa lounge. Chrome details lend sparkle to all-white baths. A sitting area in one of the suites, accented with pale touches of green and blue.

J Banks Design Group

ONE STEAMBOAT PLACE, STEAMBOAT SPRINGS, COLORADO

500,000 sf
$6 million budget (interior design)
80 owner-occupied units
Lower lobby, main lobby, members'
gathering area, spa, outdoor pool,
fitness center, and restaurant

Some designers find inspiration in art; others look to the natural world. But in the case of this resort residence in the ski town of Steamboat Springs, Joni Vanderslice and Shelley Wilkins turned to a pair of whimsically painted cowboy boots from their personal collection. To the duo from J Banks Design, a South Carolina firm known for its ecofriendly leanings, the colorful footwear symbolized being rooted in tradition but also standing as an individual—a vivid image that guided the project's execution and branding.

Decor-wise, the concept translated into the use of indigenous materials and classic southwestern hues along with earthy touches like energy-efficient lighting fixtures created by local craftsmen. Lending rough-hewn luxe are refurbished antiques, river-rock mosaics, and walls and floors sheathed in reclaimed barn wood. Artwork is plentiful, with one favorite piece being the backlit glass deer head (a funky rendition of the staid hunting trophy) that hangs proudly in the members' gathering area. Enveloping seating vignettes sprinkled throughout the public spaces, as well as an array of lush custom textiles, keep the feel residential despite the building's enormity. And while the state-of-the-art fitness room and outdoor lap pool are de rigueur for luxury resorts these days, the adjoining spa and award-winning Truffle Pig restaurant— helmed by an alum of Thomas Keller's French Laundry— reflect the property's unique flavor and flair.

Clockwise from top:
Local references abound in the main lounge, including a handblown-glass chandelier depicting a school of trout. Indigenous river rock was used for flooring in the spa, which also features a wall lined in birch branches and a desk detailed with backlit stone. The members' gathering area, with snug seating vignettes, encourages lingering and socializing. Outsize furnishings— such as nailhead-studded club chairs— bring the airy lobby lounge down to scale. A glowing glass deer head offers a cheeky take on the iconic form.

PROJECT TEAM JONI VANDERSLICE,
SHELLEY WILKINS
ARCHITECT OF RECORD RNL
PHOTOGRAPHY SHAWN O'CONNOR

www.jbanksdesign.com

HARRAH'S CHEROKEE CASINO AND RESORT—CREEK TOWER
CHEROKEE, NORTH CAROLINA

Cuningham Group Architecture

420,000 sf
$130,000,000 construction budget
454 standard guest rooms and 78 suites

*Clockwise from top:
The staggered roofline
of the 200-foot tower
evokes the nearby
mountains. Patrons
check in at a desk
fronted in stylized
river cane; the design
of the sculptural
lighting was inspired
by fire and smoke.
The lobby's wood-slat
ceiling treatment
continues into the
edgier VIP check-in
area. Rugged
stonework invites the
outdoors into the café
lounge, where window
walls supply natural
light and views of a
babbling brook.* ➤

After completing several projects on this North Carolina site, the firm returned to tackle another phase: a resort tower designed to supply the kind of artful pleasures that hip visitors might seek in Las Vegas. A contemporary lodge scheme adds even more appeal for an outdoorsy crowd drawn by the grandeur and beauty of the surrounding Smoky Mountains.

The roofline of the 21-story tower echoes the silhouette of the rolling peaks. Entering guests encounter building elements reminiscent of the forest; materials like river cane, native grasses, and rustic stonework coax Mother Nature indoors. Throughout, four stylistic themes—Mountain Breeze, Woodland Moon, River Valley, and Earth Water—are expressed via millwork and upholstery details. Plush seating, Native American art, and a fire pit create a lobby-level lounge conducive to conversation and relaxation. The ceiling above the second-floor reception suggests a canopy of trees, with shafts of light shining through gaps between the planks. Stone cladding cements the connection to the wild views visible through massive windows.

Carpets recalling a path of river stones draw guests into the playful standard guest rooms, each dressed in a red or blue color scheme. On the penthouse level are two exclusive super suites with double-height glass curtain walls providing stunning vistas. The contemporary Soho Chic Suite is a welcome wild card: One part loft, one part lodge, it's an assemblage of unexpectedly urban furnishings contrasted with plank floors and an all-glass fireplace.

Clockwise from opposite: On the 21st floor, which houses themed luxury accommodations, the Soho Chic Suite pairs slick chrome furnishings with wood floors, warm-tone textiles, and a transparent fireplace. In a standard guest room, the vanity supports a thick stone counter. Also in a standard room, the carpet design implies a path of river stones, a nod to the brook running alongside the hotel.

PROJECT TEAM THOMAS HOSKENS, DAVID HYDE, JANET WHALEY, LAURA OESTREICH, MICHELE ESPELAND

PHOTOGRAPHY PETER MALINOWSKI/INSITE (1–5), DANA WHEELOCK (6, 7)

www.cuningham.com

1 ENTRY

2 RECEPTION

3 VIP CHECK-IN

4 FIRE LOUNGE

5 CAFÉ BAKERY

0   20   40   80

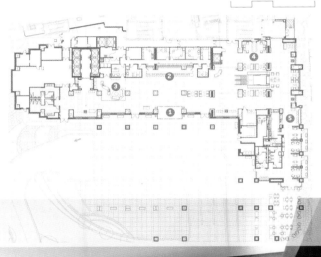

$2.55 million FF&E budget (public areas)
$8.89 million FF&E budget (guest units)

Design Group Carl Ross

HILTON GRAND WAIKIKIAN
HONOLULU, HAWAII

The California-based firm imbued this new property overlooking Waikiki Beach with a warm, welcoming touch. The idea was to meld the traditions of grand old Hawaiian hotels with the easy comfort of luxe vacation residences. More than a dozen noted Hawaiian artists contributed traditional island art: carved stone, hand-dyed tapa cloth, historical wooden weaponry, delicate feather leis. Throughout public areas are commissioned artisan-carved wood screens depicting native plants and an island legend confirmed by a local cultural advisor and consultant.

The enormous, 19,000-square-foot lobby features a reflecting pool, along with varying ceiling heights and floor patterns. Its flowing spaces—divided into passageways, vestibules, and seating areas—are unified by light fixtures, wood-plank ceilings, and the handcarved screens.

In the tower are 321 standard units and 34 penthouses. The latter employ overscale faux bois planks for flooring, handwoven area rugs, and throw pillows with coconut shell details. The chaise longue design has origins in century-old island antiques; living room media systems deliver theater-quality viewing. Master bedrooms link to baths that offer both a soaking tub and a glass-enclosed shower—indulgences befitting an oceanfront getaway.

Clockwise from above: The concierge area boasts a custom wool rug and carved panels depicting native flora. A hand-stenciled Haku Lei floral hangs over the headboard in a penthouse villa's master bedroom. The lobby elevator lounge features a bespoke wool rug and floor tiles set in a basket weave. A handcarved triptych in reception represents the spirit of native peoples' working together. The Grand Alani reception area of the 38-story tower. Granite tops the hardwood vanity and tub surround.

PROJECT TEAM CARL ROSS, JOELLE AHRENS, TAMARA SMITH, MENDY TUHTAN, CRISTIN SANBORN, LYNN HORWITZ
PHOTOGRAPHY DAVID PHELPS

www.designgroupcarlross.com

7,000,000 sf
67 treehouse villas and 26 private residences
8 spa treatment pavilions

HBA

FOUR SEASONS SEYCHELLES, MAHE

For those who dream of a distant island escape, the Seychelles offers numerous options. That's because the archipelago, in the Indian Ocean northeast of Madagascar, is composed of more than 100 granitic and coral islands. On the main island of Mahe, this sybaritic resort is perched on a hillside overlooking secluded Petite Anse Bay. HBA masterminded the interiors, designed to dazzle guests while meeting strict environmental guidelines.

The scheme takes cues from the setting, using local materials as well as a palette inspired by the nearby ocean, bamboo groves, red-tipped cinnamon trees, and fragrant frangipani. Boulders and trees removed during construction were reused, respectively, as granite cladding for walls and timber flooring for the Kannel restaurant.

Panoramic views take center stage throughout; even soaking tubs survey the island's granite peaks and azure ocean. Each spacious villa—furnished in a mix of French antiques and rustic driftwood pieces—has more living area outdoors than indoors, adding to the sense of being in a private sanctuary. The feel of a resort built into a jungle hillside is sometimes quite prevalent: The sleek interiors of many of the villas incorporate existing granite boulders, left untouched to minimize the blasting done during construction. Rock on.

Clockwise from top left: The lobby has almost entirely hardwood and timber features, while a wall of windows introduces panoramic views. A bathroom nods to the resort's landscape with sink pedestals crafted from salvaged tree trunks. A rattan ceiling and painted wood wall define a villa that opens onto a swimming pool. One of the private residential villas offers an array of natural materials and the opportunity to contemplate the Indian Ocean, visible beyond an infinity-edge pool. ➤

PROJECT TEAM CONNIE PUAR, AGNES NG, BELINDA CHIA, DULCE DILLO, JOEL JIMENEZ
ARCHITECTS OF RECORD AREA ARCHITECTS, LOCUS ARCHITECTS
PHOTOGRAPHY PETER MEALIN PHOTOGRAPHY
www.hba.com

Clockwise from left:
The pool mimics the turquoise waters of the nearby Indian Ocean, while treed granite peaks rise in the background. Views of Petite Anse Bay remain the focus in the spa relaxation lounge, where neutral furnishings are set against balau hardwood millwork. A villa's bathroom takes in ocean views; the adjoining balau deck leads to a private infinity-edge plunge pool. The library features a white-washed timber ceiling and model ships. Borrowing from nearby colonial plantations, the indoor-outdoor Kannel bar embraces more-rustic furnishings and exposed beams that blend with the surrounding greenery.

1 SPA ENTRY

2 RECEPTION

3 WAITING AREA

4 RETAIL

5 OFFICE

6 JUICE BAR

7 RELAXATION LOUNGE

0   10   20   40

$5 million FF&E budget
44 units

Design Group
Carl Ross

HYATT SIESTA KEY BEACH, FLORIDA

According to the Travel Channel, the sand beach at Florida's Siesta Key qualifies as the best in America. Which is one reason Hyatt built a six-story complex there—the tallest structure allowed—to house its second fractional residence. Visitors stay three to six weeks at a time, enjoying casual opulence on the Gulf of Mexico.

Materials and colors reflect the landscape's natural beauty. In the members' lounge, rustic planks in golden-sand tones compose the casework surrounding a large-screen television and gaming area. Onyx, limestone, granite, and travertine intermingle in a spiral pattern on the lobby and lounge floors.

The reception desktop is a two-piece diorama of sand, shells, and beach glass. The design team, in a nod to the 1950s Sarasota School movement and its late superstar architect Paul Rudolph, used horizontal slatting in the lobby. The modern-beach aesthetic carries over to guest quarters, featuring area rugs woven by hand in Thailand, shagreen-wrapped consoles, and handblown-glass lamps. Kitchens are well outfitted, with custom Italian cabinetry and appliances from the likes of Sub-Zero and Fisher & Paykel. In the master bedrooms, upholstery and curtains span a range of sunset oranges, and headboards reiterate the horizontal-slat motif.

Clockwise from above: Wood slats anchor the bed in a villa master bedroom. Poolside cabanas are dressed to the nines. The spa foyer sports woven-fabric wall covering and a handblown-glass pendant. The walls of the member's lounge are faced in driftwood-finished planks. The registration lobby features sand-and-seashell dioramas inset in the reception desk; decorative lighting is designed by Jonathan Browning Studios.

PROJECT TEAM CARL ROSS, JOELLE AHRENS, TAMARA SMITH, ALLISON SAUNDERS
PHOTOGRAPHY ROBERT MILLER
www.designgroupcarlross.com

J Banks
Design Group

THE SEBASTIAN—VAIL, COLORADO

320,000 sf
$8 million budget

*Clockwise from top:
In the library, tripod
lamps flank a canvas
by Manuel Felguérez.
Plush seating
vignettes in the back
lobby are framed by
pendant lights and
resin dividers, both
by 3-Form. Block 16
restaurant centers on
a spectacular "wine
silo" storage unit
designed with
architect Timbers
Resorts. For the front
lobby, the firm created
a concrete fireplace
and a metal-twig
chandelier that meets
local requirements for
low-wattage lighting.*

Just off the slopes in the heart of Vail Village, this boutique
resort gives traditional ski-lodge style a "mountain hip"
makeover by way of overscale proportions, nuanced color
choices, and cool custom furnishings. Perhaps the biggest
(and most expensive) aspect was removing the stone
cladding from the existing lobby fireplace and replacing it
with concrete "logs." Overhead, the metal-twig chandelier,
like all the feature lighting, was custom-designed for
energy efficiency. Pale gray and slate-blue touches recall
the brilliance of ice, snow, and sky, as do stainless-steel
accents. Black was layered in as a foil for leather and
stained-wood finishes.

The Hilton Head–based designers divided the rear lobby
with birch-framed resin panels to bring intimacy to the
soaring space. For additional coziness, they converted a
former office area into a library featuring custom millwork
and a selection of books reflecting the mountain landscape
and the interests of the clientele. Photography and other
works by local artisans complement the owners' collection
of paintings by noted Mexican abstractionist Manuel
Felguérez. These days, however, it's not just their art that's
in residence: The owners themselves were so taken with
the redo, they decided to spend part of each year here.

PROJECT TEAM JONI VANDERSLICE,
LISA WHITLEY
ARCHITECT OF RECORD TIMBERS RESORTS
PHOTOGRAPHY COURTESY TIMBERS RESORTS
www.jbanksdesign.com

Wilson Butler Architects

SOLSTICE CLASS SHIPS
FOR CELEBRITY CRUISE LINES

When tapped to create Solstice, a new luxury class for the cruise-ship giant, WBA soon had concepts in mind: simple and elegant, as unique and intimate as a boutique hotel, with a color scheme and materials suggestive of fine yachts. The route of the line—which departs from Port Everglades—would figure also, as would the ever-changing weather.

Master planner and lead design firm for the five-ship project, WBA envisioned that the spaces would reflect the beauty of the world at sea—in particular, the Greek Isles and the coastal regions of the Mediterranean, among its destinations. That is how white canvas, a boating staple, became the backdrop for warm beige stones, timeless teak, crisp blues of sky and water, and spicy accents.

Individual palettes were specified with an area's purpose in mind. The Solstice deck, a haven for sun worshipers, features intimate groupings of furniture in a hot, sunny scheme. The pool deck, with its relieving shade and varied lounging opportunities, was rendered in cool restful hues. In the glass-roof solarium, where a waterfall and fountain anchor the space, natural tones were used. And at the Lawn Club, the cheekily named sports deck, a biomorphic white canopy and actual grass—a true luxury on the high seas—set the scene.

From top: Solar panels on the glass solarium roof supplement energy and filter light; the space is anchored by a waterfall and laminar fountain. A bold floral carpet lends punch to one of the dining options, Bistro on Five. Glass-encased pillars veiled with gauzy drapes illuminate the grand foyer atrium. ➤

2,850-plus occupancy
$770 million budget

Clockwise from top:
The grand foyer, which extends upward through the four-story atrium, connects an array of dining and retail spaces. The Solstice theater, a jewel box of a venue. On the pool deck, two-level canopies double the amount of shade and privacy. Swooping canvas sail fabric provides partial cover for activities at the live-grass Lawn Club. Generous wicker daybeds with Sunbrella cushions furnish the adult sunbathing and relaxation zone, the Solstice deck.

PROJECT TEAM SCOTT BUTLER, SCOTT WILSON, TOM HAINS,
KEVIN NASTASIA, JESSICA POWELL, BARBARA SHERMAN, CHRIS DYNIA,
REBECCA EMANUEL, JESSIE BOUDREAU
BUILDER MEYER WERFT YARDS
PHOTOGRAPHER ROBERT BENSON PHOTOGRAPHY

www.wilsonbutler.com

1 PANORAMIC LIFTS
2 STAGE
3 WET ZONE
4 FAMILY POOL
5 SPORTS POOL
6 POOL BAR
7 RETAIL
8 SOLARIUM POOL
9 SPA CAFÉ
10 AQUA SPA

0 10 20 50

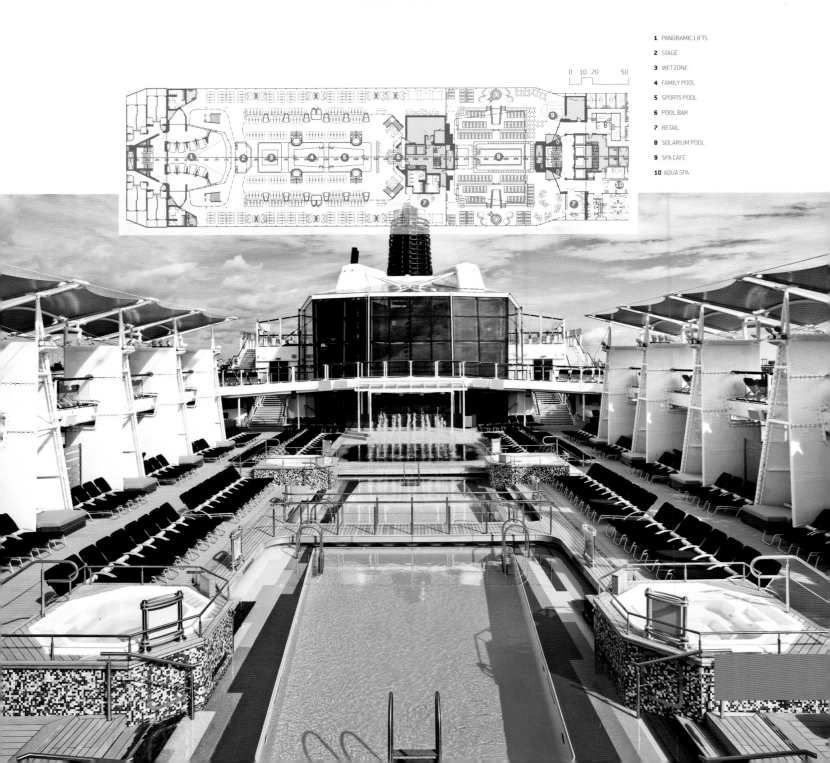

BraytonHughes Design Studios
and Hornberger + Worstell

**THE RITZ-CARLTON
LAKE TAHOE, CALIFORNIA**

This upscale property represents a seamless collaboration between interior design and architecture, nature and the manmade. At its heart is an octagonal lobby that pays tribute to the great mountain lodges of the West via a soaring 55-foot-tall fireplace and chimney of weathered granite. Surrounding windows frame views of the forest, meadows, and ski slopes. Those vistas, in turn, suggested an interiors palette of gold, red, green, and Sierra blue that reads differently depending on the season.

The native flora also inspired motifs for custom carpets and curtains. A collection of art by locals further brings in the Lake Tahoe landscape, and many furnishings were made by area artisans using regionally sourced materials. Cedar-plank

woodwork and alpine-green slate flooring were also found nearby, helping the property become one of the first five-star mountain resorts certified as LEED Silver. (Low-VOC paints, GreenGuard-certified carpets, and energy-efficient light fixtures contributed, too.)

Guest rooms have ecofriendly gas fireplaces and are extra wide to allow for generous fenestration. Layouts betray the designers' residential perspective, with a wood-clad foyer and a lounge area furnished with custom leather club chairs for in-room fireside dining. The hearth, closets, desk, and other amenities are neatly integrated into one wall. And bathrooms come equipped with decadent soaking tubs. Forget cabin fever; who'd ever want to leave?

From top: Lodgelike residential suites boast gas-burning fireplaces, energy-efficient (and insulating) double-pane windows, and wood-beam ceilings. In the airy grand lobby, floored in green slate, custom furniture, millwork, and carpets carve out cozy seating areas; walls have weathered-granite wainscoting. ➤

PROJECT TEAMS BRAYTONHUGHES DESIGN STUDIOS: STANFORD HUGHES, LAURA COOK, KRIS KAWAII TORAL, MEGHAN LOPEZ. HORNBERGER + WORSTELL: MARK HORNBERGER, JOHN DAVIS, CHRIS APICELLA

PHOTOGRAPHY CHRIS CYPERT/CYPERT AND LEONG

www.bhdstudios.com

Clockwise from left:
Daylight floods in through the lobby's 25-foot-high double-pane windows; the carpet's leaf design was sparked by the evergreens right outside. The space flows around a freestanding stacked-granite hearth. The spa's wood-paneled lounge is capped by a dome that's octagonal, as is the hotel lobby.

170 keys
Two adjacent buildings with 23 residences, a 17,000-square-foot spa, and a function space with a 6,000-square-foot ballroom

0 10 20   40

1 ENTRY

2 RECEPTION

3 LOUNGE AREAS

4 FIREPLACE

5 DINING AREA

spa & beauty

Facilities offering deep-tissue massages, sea-salt scrubs, and oxygen facials aren't the only spaces getting the spa treatment. These days, designers are expected to bring a pampering, sybaritic touch to project types ranging from health clubs to hair salons.

At the top of the services menu is, of course, blissful relaxation. Hence the emphasis on natural light, outdoor views, and transporting water features. In an effort to establish a soothing atmosphere, designers are looking beyond the usual Far Eastern motifs (although those work wonderfully, too), dreaming up spaces that play against type, subverting expectations. Witness Revel spa's industrial-chic interior, a scheme both budget-conscious and ecofriendly (terms not usually associated with high-end spas). Or take Oak Bay, which offers exercise facilities in a faux British castle. Then there's George the Salon, a spare, elemental aerie that proves decadence need not involve grand gestures. Sometimes the biggest luxury is a quiet design detail enabling superior service. *Lean back, put your feet up, and...ahhh.*

REVEL SPA, SAN FRANCISCO

Jiun Ho

Crisp white walls and weathered wood are two hallmarks
of this deceptively simple spa with a Vietnamese twist.
Close scrutiny reveals ingenious details: A cluster of vintage
birdcages hangs from a ceiling arrangement of crisscrossed
worn planks; inside some cages, a single lightbulb dangles.
Carved tabletop finials could have been plucked from
the remains of an ancient religious shrine. A sleek swath
of stained oak starts at the ceiling only to evolve into a
manicure table below.

Because the spa is sparingly adorned, each object takes
on greater meaning, and the contrast of clean and modern
with rustic and venerable imparts a kind of timeless,
unfussy serenity. For artwork, the designer used his own
photographs, taken in his homeland of Vietnam. The
oversize landscapes and scenes of working people provide
a welcome departure from the expected, signaling as they
do a peaceful escape tempered with realism.

That Jiun Ho considered feng shui principles in designing
the interior comes as little surprise. A distinct feeling
of spaciousness permeates—all views and paths are
clear—and soothes the spirit. One senses that as in a good
poem, all that *needs* to be is here...and not an iota more.

Clockwise from opposite: *A Burmese Buddha presides from its niche over the drying station; George Nelson chairs serve as seating. The flooring in reception is epoxy. A flock of abstract bird sculptures flies across a wall in the lower-level waiting area; each winged piece is reclaimed metal hand-dipped in white acrylic. Sleek manicure stations snake across the undisguised ceiling and down the wall.* ➤

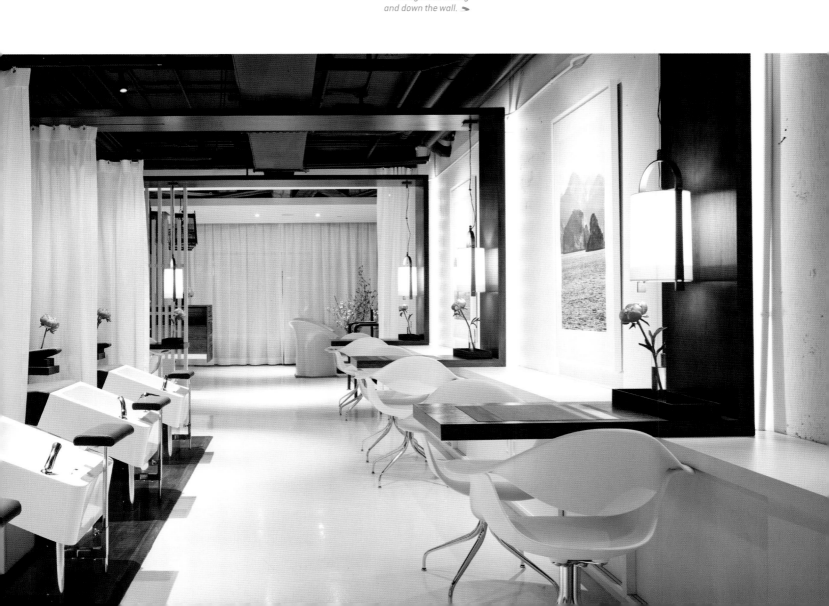

Clockwise from top left: A grouping of birdcages hovers over the weathered-oak reception desk. In this treatment room and elsewhere, the designer's own photographs supply an authentic, unromanticized touch. The view across the nail salon is a study in symmetry, down to the flowers; scrims neatly divide stations. Glass railings enlarge the range of vision as well as the space; the stairs are rugged concrete. Teak paneling—salvaged from an old Thai house—lines the wall behind a handcrafted vanity.

2,800 sf
4 treatment rooms

PROJECT TEAM JIUN HO, JENN RADLINSKI
PHOTOGRAPHY BRUCE DAMONTE
www.jiunho.com

This restful haven overlooks the turquoise expanse of Kapalua Bay on Maui's northern coast, on a site verdant with palm trees, tropical flora, and luxuriant grasses. That lushness informed every aspect of the interior scheme, from the soothing mix of blues and greens to the architecture's fluid relationship between indoors and out.

The sprawling spa boasts myriad spaces for healing and pampering: 19 single treatment rooms, 10 outdoor massage hales (complete with private soaking tubs), an oceanfront gym, sauna and steam rooms, a beauty salon, a saltwater lap pool, and more. Despite its massive scale, though, the space feels intimate and personal courtesy of a design that re-creates the ambience of a breezy modern beach house. The building has the feel of a series of interconnected villas that embrace the outdoors via walls that dissolve to access private decks, bamboo groves, fragrant gardens, water features, and ocean vistas. Natural materials throughout were inspired by the Hawaiian coastline—textured stones, woven fabrics, river-rock mosaics, and surfaces inlaid with seashells and beach glass.

Philpotts Interiors
KAPALUA SPA, MAUI, HAWAII

30,000 sf
29 treatment rooms

PROJECT TEAM JONATHON STAUB
ARCHITECT OF RECORD WCIT
PHOTOGRAPHY FRANZEN PHOTOGRAPHY
www.philpotts.net

Clockwise from opposite top:
A chandelier of cascading glass orbs hangs from a gridlike wood-plank ceiling in the lobby, which offers ocean views. A treatment room's teak-clad shower has basalt flooring and walls of ashlar-patterned tumbled-glass mosaic. Bleached mahogany envelops a massage room in an outdoor cabana; the counter-top is reclaimed glass. Also outdoors, an oversize rain shower opens onto a private garden shaded by a bamboo trellis. The architecture marries Hawaiian vernacular and clean-lined modernism. A carved-stone sink fills via a waterfall spout.

2,000 sf
8 styling stations

GEORGE THE SALON, CHICAGO

When celebrity hairstylist George Gonzalez set out to open his own salon, he tapped De Shun Wang to not only design the space but also assist in the real-estate hunt. Their search for a well-situated but tranquil downtown location led to a fourth-floor loft with generous north-facing windows and four skylights. Alas, the plethora of brick walls—though possessing a certain charm—made conditions darker and less sleek than desired.

A new open-plan layout emphasizes the ample daylight while warm wood finishes and whitewashed walls answer the request for a luxurious yet welcoming modern environment. The brick window wall was Sheetrocked over to tone down the industrial vibe while a ceiling canopy frames the apertures overhead so they read as fixtures. "Those skylights are better than chandeliers," notes Wang. All furnishings are custom, from the waiting area's built-in banquette to the dark-stained oak-veneer styling stations. A huge mirror at each station seems to enlarge its square footage and performs a kind of social role, too. "It's more than just a reflective surface," the designer explains. "The size of the mirror enhances communication between stylist and patron, allowing the latter to give the salon its true personality."

DW Design Workshop

Clockwise from opposite: A custom banquette defines the waiting lounge, where a recessed retail display exploits narrow confines. Styling stations built from oak-veneer shelving support mirrors framed in stainless steel and bracketed by low-color temperature incandescent tubes. Granite tops the check-in desk. The salon is floored in Brazilian cherry and illuminated via skylights and recessed fixtures.

PROJECT TEAM DE SHUN WANG, CHING FENG LI

PHOTOGRAPHY KAT FILIPINAS

www.dwdw.co

29,800 sf
Gym, basketball court,
pool, hot tub, and juice bar

ISSI Design
OAK BAY CLUBHOUSE, FUZHOU, CHINA

This high-end fitness center on China's southeast coast has a somewhat unlikely inspiration: a grand English castle. Patrician touches like figured millwork, fine artwork, and glittery chandeliers create an atmosphere that might seem more suited to sporting than sports. But where you'd expect to find ballrooms and dining parlors, there's a basketball court and a juice bar.

En route to the athletic facilities, patrons navigate a majestic lobby whose skylit celestial-blue ceiling makes the space even more loftlike. Exposed-brick walls are accented with rotary-cut bubinga beams, which have been treated to a high-gloss piano finish. The stately environs are warmed by the glow of chandeliers as well as a sentry of life-size horse lamps whose theme reappears in a large-scale painting of red-coated huntsmen pursuing game.

Windows in the second-floor gym look onto the pool below; their painted sashes and bars recall Asian sliding screens. The swimming area is lined with white marble columns that lend a decidedly old-world aura. A yachtlike ceiling seemingly made of rich teak turns out to be faux bois PVC. This treatment is repeated in the more intimate Jacuzzi area, where a circular tub sits amid walls faced in gold ceramic tiles—a final royal touch.

Clockwise from above: Faux bois PVC faces the sloped ceiling above the pool, whose columns were inspired by a plaza square. A view of the lobby ceiling. In the entryway, bronze chandeliers and sconces are joined by a herd of horse lamps by Swedish design collective Front. A corridor lined with red grid windows overlooks the pool. The Jacuzzi area is swathed in ceramic tile.

PROJECT TEAM ANDY LEUNG,
HENRY HAN, QIAN FENG

PHOTOGRAPHY IN-FOTOS STUDIO

www.issi-design.com

fine dining

In a fine-dining establishment, a meal is a multisensory indulgence; the flavor and aroma of the cuisine is just the beginning. Design is also integral to the experience, tantalizing patrons' sense of sight and, especially, touch.

Whether the interior is spare and ethereal or rustic and earthy, texture provides a sense of richness via nubby linen drapes, sculptural door handles, cushy velvet upholstery, or buttery leather wall treatments. Diners want to be cosseted. But they also want to be included in the action—thus the recent vogue for exposing back-of-the-house magic. Windows might provide teasing views into a prep area, whereas exhibition-style kitchens transform the ritual of cooking into full-blown theater. Other sight lines are considered, too: Take in Fiola's contemporary photographs or the Ingres-inspired mosaics at Felix. And when the eatery is located in a museum, why not highlight pieces from the permanent collection or, in the case of the Wright, commission one for it? *Exhibition style, indeed.*

It was a tall order, to put it mildly: Redo a restaurant—within a New York art institution designed by Frank Lloyd Wright—to reference the building's signature ramp without hewing too closely to it. As if that wasn't pressure enough, the eatery would be named for the late architect himself.

Fortunately, Andre Kikoski was up to the task of renovating the Solomon R. Guggenheim Museum's ground-floor restaurant as part of the 50th-anniversary celebration. In choosing the ceiling as the site for Wright's focal point, Kikoski essentially turned the concept on its head. The spiraling layers of stretched membrane above give visitors a sense of having entered the mouth of a giant nautilus shell. His palette stays true to the Guggenheim's as well, without being derivative—meaningful color erupts on the largely white interior, much as Ellsworth Kelly's canvases once did on the gallery walls.

Of course art is at the heart of the project. An installation by sculptor Liam Gillick, done in collaboration with Kikoski, contributes the majority of color. Stacked aluminum planks in staggered shades of yellow, orange, red, and gray wrap the swooping wall above a vivid blue banquette. Beside the original glass entryway hangs a companion piece: Commissioned for the permanent collection, it provides privacy without hemming in the snug space.

Andre Kikoski Architect

THE WRIGHT, NEW YORK

1,600 sf
58 seats

PROJECT TEAM ANDRE KIKOSKI, BRIAN LEWIS, GUNNAR JUNG, ADAM DARTER, LIAM HARRIS, CLAIRE FOY, LAURIE KARSTEN
PHOTOGRAPHY PETER AARON/OTTO
www.akarch.com

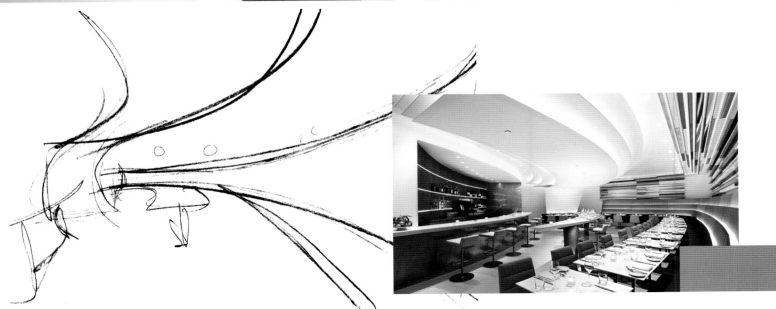

Dreamtime Australia Design

CONCRETE BLONDE, SYDNEY

The Potts Point area has long been Sydney's bohemian hub. Over the past few years, however, it has experienced a wave of new business, drawing a swish crowd that hobnobs among the Art Deco apartment buildings and Victorian houses. Concrete Blonde lures those trendy buzz-seekers with its cutting-edge, style-driven approach.

The design team preserved the site's industrial grid of concrete beams and exposed hydraulic pipes but warmed the vibe with oak tables, plate-steel gas fireplaces, bar-top table lamps, and copious candles. Acoustic flocking made of recycled paper dampens noise, and stainless-steel-mesh panels cover recessed areas of the ceiling for a more enveloping feel. Cement-fiber sheeting lining horizontal surfaces in the main dining area lends texture, as does an accent wall behind the bar, clad in driftwood planks that are embedded with steel nails. Multiple nooks are available—both indoors and out—for year-round canoodling.

Providing the theatrical center is an open exhibition kitchen equipped with a circular wood-fired rotisserie and two gas-fueled char grills. The 26-foot-long communal dining table and a stainless-steel bar (complete with DJ booth) offer hip diners opportunities for intense interaction while they sample Clarence River prawns or housemade potato gnocchetti with edamame and sweet corn.

4,175 sf
140 seats

PROJECT TEAM MICHAEL MC CANN, SALLY GORDON, CRISTINA LUPICA

PHOTOGRAPHY PAUL GOSNEY

www.dreamtimeaustraliadesign.com

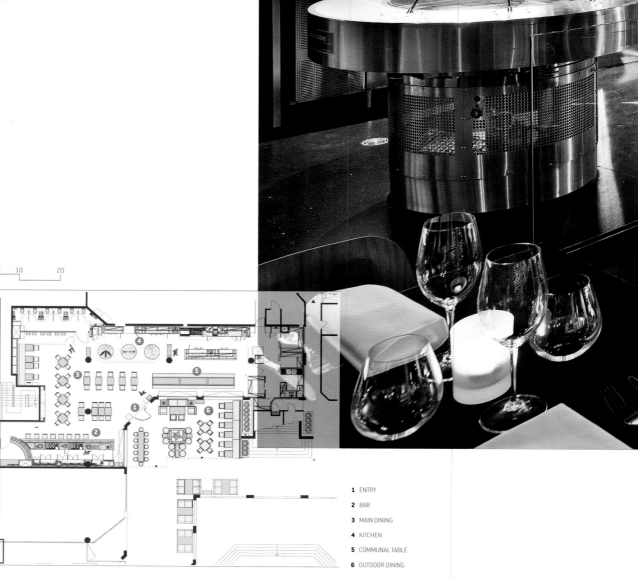

Clockwise from top:
The communal table has integrated light fixtures and a view of the alfresco dining area. Patrons can see chefs prepare their food in the open kitchen from a phalanx of molded-plywood Eames chairs and custom tables; firewood is stored in stainless-steel cylinders. Plate-steel box shelving displays wine bottles.

0   5   10   20

1 ENTRY

2 BAR

3 MAIN DINING

4 KITCHEN

5 COMMUNAL TABLE

6 OUTDOOR DINING

SHANG PALACE AND LI BAI LOUNGE
TAIPEI, TAIWAN

AB Concept

Located on the sixth floor of the Shangri-La Far Eastern Plaza Hotel, this atmospheric restaurant and lounge unspools via a series of wood-paneled corridors and moodily lit rooms. The seductive layout not only tantalizes guests but also helps distract from spatial challenges—namely low ceilings and an irregular floor plate.

Chinese iconography informs many details. A wall relief behind the maître d' stand is shaped like a celestial cloud, an ancient Asian motif. To the left is the lounge—inspired by Tang Dynasty romantic poet Li Bai—which channels a traditional Chinese scholar's pavilion by way of dark-wood finishes, muted lighting, and a ceiling layered with distressed-pine panels. The restaurant is reached by the "tea alley," a gallery lined with zigzagging oak doors that conceal storage. Bronze partitions divide the dining area into a series of intimate zones, serving to de-emphasize the modest headroom. The celestial cloud theme crops up again in a plaster ceiling relief as well as in upholstery and carpet patterns. And four private dining areas spiral around a skylit circular foyer clad in wood fins arrayed to form a stylized peony, a symbol of good fortune.

Clockwise from top:
A close-up of the cloud-shape alcove behind reception, built from interlit layers of timber treated with pearlescent paint. The peony-inspired skylight in the circular vestibule servicing private dining is lined with 6½-foot-long bronze-tipped wood panels. Oak doors with blown-glass pulls and bronze accents line the tea alley, which leads to the restaurant. ➤

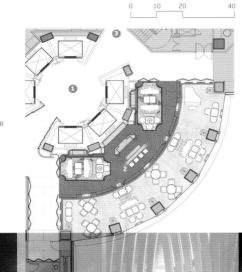

9,688 sf
55 seats (lounge)

Clockwise from opposite: On the tea alley ceiling are concave ceramic tiles whose curves are echoed in the hand-tufted carpet. Suspended silk lanterns bracket the maître d' stand. Bronze screens inset with purple-glass medallions create cozy seating areas. The pine panels bordering the metallic-painted lounge ceiling were distressed with a wire brush.

PROJECT TEAM ED NG, TERENCE NGAN
PHOTOGRAPHY CHESTER ONG
www.abconcept.net

1 ELEVATOR CORRIDOR

2 LOUNGE

3 RESTAURANT

Tucked inside Chicago's landmark Belden-Stratford hotel, in ritzy Lincoln Park, is the calmly luxurious seafood restaurant L2O. The interior, by principal Dirk Denison, is a deliberately soothing departure from the hotel's hustle-bustle. Customers pass through a set of impressive ebony doors into a serene entry foyer defined by a dense grouping of Macassar ebony columns. A few steps down is the dining zone, delineated by etched-glass panels and taut stainless-steel cables stretched floor to ceiling. The palette—a sea of black, white, caramel, and straw—emanates a Zen-like calm.

Here, and in a lounge that opens off the main space, circular ebony tables seem to float above sleek cantilevered white-leather chairs. Along the restaurant's rear wall, niches lined in onyx and velvet form romantic nooks. Among the private dining areas is a tatami room furnished with traditional straw-mat floor coverings and sunken tables crafted from yellow cedar; sliding shoji screens carve up the space into smaller zones.

Even the back of house, whose intense activity is carefully guarded, is designed with high-quality finishes—compliments to the chef.

Dirk Denison Architects

L20 RESTAURANT, CHICAGO

PHOTOGRAPHY MICHELLE LITVIN

www.dirkdenisonarchitects.com

136 seats
Gold Key Award grand-
prize winner, Fine Dining

Main dining room, 2 private
dining rooms, and 3 semiprivate
dining areas

Clockwise from opposite top: Custom glass chandeliers cast a glow on walls clad in blond sen-wood veneer. Flexible furnishings and movable screens allow the private tatami room to be configured for two to eight guests. Macassar ebony columns define the raised entry. An artwork by Scott Short enlivens a seating nook. Glass panels partially obscure a small lounge and private dining room from the entry. Near custom serving gueridons, a curtain of stainless-steel cables creates subtle separation.

Federico Delrosso Architects

2,400 sf (restaurant)
1,600 sf (rooftop lounge)

Clockwise from above: PVC tubes form an ornamental canopy over the host station at CaféB. A neutral palette leaves the focus on the food. A digitally printed photomural of library bookshelves distinguishes a corner outfitted with a painted-wood table and trattoria lighting by Massimiliano and Raffaele Alajmo. ➤

CAFÉB RESTAURANT + SKYB ROOFTOP LOUNGE, NEW YORK

Federico Delrosso had already designed two outposts of the venerable restaurant brand Bice—in San Diego and Istanbul—when he was enlisted to tackle a new location, at New York's Hotel Indigo. The architect conceived the stylish eatery as a love letter to Milan, the capital of contemporary Italian design—and, he notes, the aperitif.

Delrosso re-created the vibe of Milanese social life with open-plan spaces that flow together like a series of terraces; the casual layout encourages the eye to wander. Quiet tones of dark brown and warm beige were deemed not only suitably urbane but also the ideal backdrop for the eatery's richly colored cuisine. Almost every element of the decor is made in Italy, from the collection of black-and-white photos to the lamps by designer Davide Groppi.

The ground-floor CaféB has what the architect calls an "alter ego" in SkyB. This rooftop terrace is even more informal and unstructured, with a floorplan inspired by urban piazzas. Low-slung furnishings keep the emphasis on the panoramic skyline, visible as soon as guests step off the elevator. For seating, Delrosso specified his own beanbag chaises and elemental folded-aluminum chairs, which he describes as being "sculptural without feeling invasive." (Both are manufactured by the Italian brand Extra, which also produced the café's stools and host station.) Glass panes along the perimeter are fritted with a gradient pattern that fogs at the base—dissolving the boundaries between architecture and cityscape, indoors and out, Manhattan and Milano.

1 ELEVATOR LOBBY/ENTRY

2 RESTROOM

3 FRONT TERRACE

4 BAR

5 BACK TERRACE

Clockwise from opposite top: The L-shape rooftop lounge SkyB is furnished with Delrosso's powder-coated aluminum seats and faux-leather beanbag chaises. Fritted glass wind-breaks protect the terrace. Brick walls were hidden behind patinated pine planks. A forest of PVC tubing screens one wall. The lounge overlooks iconic water towers on nearby Chelsea rooftops.

PROJECT TEAM FEDERICO DELROSSO, DARIO DE SANTIS, SARA FOSCHI, EDA KOKSAL

GENERAL CONTRACTOR ITALIAN FINEST CUSTOM CREATIONS

PHOTOGRAPHY ADRIAN WILSON

www.federicodelrosso.com

DH Design Studio

THE FARM, PARK CITY, UTAH

This restaurant is situated in the center of a ski-resort village. Yet, despite the alpine setting, the designers deliberately dodged mountain-theme clichés in favor of urbane refinement, quietly nodding to the locale via an array of indigenous natural finishes. The materials selection also reflects the menu's emphasis on seasonal fare, regional organic produce, and meats sourced from purveyors based within 100 miles.

A light-washed wall swathed in end-grain oak tiles defines the entry. Opposite is a dramatic curved partition—capped with a countertop of rare wood-stone—that's partially open to the restaurant beyond, offering views into the stainless-steel exhibition kitchen. Mirroring the wave shape is a serving station built into a high-back semicircular banquette. Other patrons relax in classic camelback side chairs, metal-framed leather seats, or the adjacent bar/lounge's red-mohair club chairs. Here, an array of intriguing features fosters a warm, inviting mood: There's a tiger's-eye granite countertop, a backlit metal cabinet with glass pocket doors, and a floor-to-ceiling wine cabinet housing 864 bottles—a panoply to choose from after a brisk day on the slopes.

Clockwise from top: The full-height wine cabinet doubles as a design element. A wall near the entry is treated to a mosaic of wax-finish end-grain oak blocks lit by fixtures hidden behind vertical planks. Earthy notes prevail in restrooms, too. Exposed-wood finishes achieve a balance of rugged and refined in the Farm's bar/lounge. Club chairs are covered in mohair.

3,650 sf
80 seats

PROJECT TEAM REBECCA BUCHAN, MICHELE WHEELER, MATT DICKAMORE
PHOTOGRAPHY DAVID NEWKIRK
www.dentonhouse.com

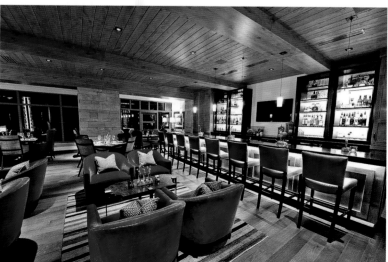

DB BISTRO MODERNE, VANCOUVER, B.C.

In designing a Canadian outpost of Daniel Boulud's popular Manhattan bistro, JansonGoldstein faced a challenge typical of restaurant rollouts: how to create a decor that captures the new location's unique flavor yet references the character of the original. The solution? Giving the brand's urbane French style a relaxed, outdoorsy spin by way of refined but rustic finishes and furnishings.

A palette of leather, stone, and patinated wood knits together the free-flowing space. Entry is made through the bar, where a soft glow emanates from hand-poured glass orbs based on a 1960s Italian lighting design. Rich texture is abundant: There are linen drapes, travertine floor planks arrayed in a herringbone pattern, a zinc countertop, and an accent wall surfaced in a basket weave of polished stainless-steel strips framed by red eel-skin.

A sawtooth-texture bronze-glass partition screens the bar from DB Bistro Moderne's main dining area. The room is lit by a series of rolled-steel fixtures that read like dashes across the ceiling. Patrons sit in distressed-oak chairs or banquettes upholstered in chocolate-brown or copper-colored woven leather. In the 16-seat private dining area at the rear, the material repeats as a wall treatment in the form of running-bond-patterned tiles. Full-height wine racks crafted from oil-quenched steel bracket the intimate retreat—a relaxing spot indeed to enjoy haute bistro fare.

Clockwise from top:
A detail of the zinc bar-top. The cast-glass partition separating the bar and dining areas echoes the texture of the hostess stand, built from European walnut. Wine bottles are stored in custom bronze racks in the private dining room, whose walls are surfaced in leather tiles. In the main dining room, custom chairs upholstered in distressed leather flank European oak tables; the backlit wall sculpture alternates grooved cast glass, bronzed mirror, and red lacquer. Chef Boulud at work.

2,000 sf
100 seats (dining room), 20 (bar)

JansonGoldstein

PROJECT TEAM HAL GOLDSTEIN, VICTORIA NADY, MARY POLITES
PHOTOGRAPHY EVAAN KHERAJ
www.jansongoldstein.com

Dreamtime Australia Design

FELIX, SYDNEY

The classic French brasserie served as a starting point for this sybaritic restaurant on one of the city's few remaining pedestrian-only laneways. The design team took a few tasteful liberties with the genre, however, layering in elements that bring Deco and Art Nouveau style squarely into this millennium.

Leather banquettes, cast-iron tables, rattan chairs, and subway-tile walls provide the familiar, while a series of arty custom details lends a contemporary twist. The facade of the 1880s building is shaded by crimson awnings whose undersides are silkscreened with reproductions of Jean-Honoré Fragonard landscapes. Blue-chip touches continue inside: The subject of Jean-Auguste Ingres's *La Grand Odalisque*, rendered in a black-and-white mosaic of hand-cut glass, reposes in the kitchen. The same medium was used to create the bar's garden-party frieze—of frolicking nudes—by local artist Sally Spratt.

A wine cellar that runs the length of the dining area is detailed like a family heirloom, with carved gargoyle heads and claw feet. Evoking luxury train travel of yore, a leather banquette topped with antique brass-wire luggage racks separates the dining area from the bar. There, a 30-foot-long pewter counter is flanked by a pair of outsize cast-aluminum urns with built-in uplighting to showcase ice-cold bottles of bubbly. Theatrical touches aside, Felix is grounded by the warm glow of brass table lamps with gold-tasseled red shades. And by its signature offerings: oysters and Champagne.

Clockwise from above: Stack-back accordion windows of beveled glass fold open so guests can dine alfresco at rattan chairs and cast-iron tables. Visible beyond the luggage-rack room divider is the handcrafted bar, anchored by 32-inch-diameter Champagne urns illuminated from within. The custom glass-mosaic reproduction of La Grand Odalisque. ➤

1 ENTRY

2 BAR/LOUNGE

3 WINE WALL

4 OYSTER BAR

5 MAIN DINING

6 KITCHEN

7 COOL ROOM

0   10   20   40

PROJECT TEAM MICHAEL MC CANN, SALLY GORDON, KATHRYN ASHLEY
PHOTOGRAPHY PAUL GOSNEY
www.dreamtimeaustraliadesign.com

Clockwise from top:
French oak lines the
dining room ceiling;
past the central
leather banquette,
whose custom lamp
features gold filigree
tassels, is the timber-
clad oyster bar. The
visage of Felix's owner
was playfully cast
onto the Champagne
urns. Onyx panels
separate sections of
the wine cellar. The
grape-cluster handles
are custom. Subway-
tile walls decorate the
main dining area,
where guests sit
on classic Thonet
bistro chairs. A bronze
logo set into the
entry's Calacatta
marble floor. Kitchen
walls dressed in
mosaics repeat
the curtained
background from
La Grand Odalisque.

Dirk Denison Architects

TERZO PIANO RESTAURANT, CHICAGO

8,500 sf
250 seats
Gold Key Award finalist

The architect's design for this restaurant, located in the Art Institute of Chicago's Modern Wing, brings the museum experience straight into the dining area. Vitrines throughout the airy, loftlike eatery display rotating artworks from the permanent collection, providing both character and loose spatial borders.

Another boundary is established by a curved garde-manger near the entry that serves as a buffer between the public terrace and restaurant. The painted-metal pod—a satellite food-prep station—was a by-product of building restrictions that dictated the unusually long distance between the kitchen and dining areas. Adjacent to it is a separate volume housing the bar, wine and cheese display, beverage service, and wine room—all slightly set off from the otherwise open-plan space.

Food service is lunch only, so full-height windows take advantage of natural daylight, as does the armada of white seating by George Nelson and Arne Jacobsen. Tabletops are white resin, which glows and reflects the shifting light throughout the day. In the evenings, the restaurant hosts banquets and private events, necessitating flexibility in capacity, furniture arrangement, and vibe. Long runs of banquettes backed by credenzas are actually a series of smaller units, poised on casters for easy repositioning. The predominance of creamy hues also means that the space, like a white-box gallery, can be dressed as desired—and is therefore ever changing.

PHOTOGRAPHY MICHELLE LITVIN

www.dirkdenisonarchitects.com

Clockwise from top:
Anchored by a garde-manger, the entry lounge features Mies van der Rohe's iconic chairs and daybed. The reconfigurable dining area, here set for the daily lunch service, is furnished with George Nelson Swag Leg chairs. The bright third-floor restaurant has a view of nearby Millennium Park and Lake Michigan. Art displays are interspersed throughout. Arne Jacobsen Series 7 stools await guests at the white marble bar.

FIOLA, WASHINGTON, D.C.

"We knew we were in for a challenge when our clients chose a cursed space," quips principal Griz Dwight, describing a site that had housed five restaurants in ten years and remained vacant for the last two. Adding insult to injury, four of said eateries were Italian in concept—the very same cuisine planned for Fiola. "We were faced with resurrecting a restaurant graveyard," he deadpans.

The renovation began with an exorcism of sorts, as the design team stripped back the layers of failed concepts to reveal the bones of the space. The fatal flaw became immediately clear: There were three slightly different floor levels—an awkward feature further accentuated by partitions that obscured views, caused service glitches, and generally made the space unpleasant.

GrizForm placed the bar on the top level and built up the lowest portion to create a single dining floor, thus improving the flow of energy, patrons, and waitstaff. Finishes were chosen to complement the menu's balance of rustic and luxurious Italian ingredients. Golden onyx mosaic floors, glass chandeliers, and glossy rosewood walls evoke the grandeur of a Tuscan villa while the bar's distressed-copper panels, live-edge-wood drink rails, leaf-patterned glass columns, and stone-clad walls speak to the Umbrian landscape. Given the chic and buzz-worthy results, it seems the curse has finally been lifted.

Clockwise from top: In the lounge, a Deborah Paauwe photograph is set off by sustainably harvested rosewood-veneer paneling. The dining room features a gilded barrel-vaulted ceiling, onyx mosaic floor, rosewood tabletops, and leather-upholstered seating. Bisecting the bar is a column clad in channel glass with embedded silk leaves. Windows in a stone-faced wall offer views into the kitchen. In the lounge, bubble-glass chandeliers dangle from gold-leaf vaulted pockets.

3,900 sf
$825,000 budget
216 seats

GrizForm
Design Architects

PROJECT TEAM GRIZ DWIGHT, MICHELLE BOVÉ, BROOKE LOEWEN

PHOTOGRAPHY PAUL BURK PHOTOGRAPHY

www.grizform.com

casual dining

While "casual" may imply a certain informality, there's nothing nonchalant about the delectable design of these eateries.

Indeed, it takes a lot of effort, creativity, and fine-tuning to achieve just the right note of laid-back comfort—and to balance that chill vibe with smart touches befitting a high-style destination. Such an undertaking is made even trickier when the restaurant in question is an amenity of a larger facility—a café or food court within, say, a retail space, resort, or office building. In such cases, the restaurant must perform a dual role: offering a cohesive sense of place while somehow referencing the architectural context and/or locale. Oftentimes, the challenge entails envisioning a decor that encourages diners to linger yet abets the complex choreography of takeout traffic in a snug footprint. Accordingly, many of the following projects take advantage of the interior envelope, transforming wall and ceiling planes into striking accents (and branding opportunities) that don't consume lots of floor space. *Talk about having your cake and eating it too.*

CCS Architecture

SANDTON SUN HOTEL
JOHANNESBURG, SOUTH AFRICA

Architect Cass Calder Smith had a lot on his plate in creating the dining venues of this South African hotel. The project, a collaboration with restaurant consultant Adam Block, encompassed six interconnected eateries— from a business lounge to a casual all-day café—totaling 15,000 square feet. The challenge was to unify the spaces while giving each a distinct look, a goal he accomplished by adhering to a concise palette of locally sourced materials. Zebrawood, oak, quartzite, and sandstone appear throughout, creating cohesion as patrons move from grilled steak at Vin mmx—a fine-dining establishment complete with cheese room—to late-night cocktails at San Bar. The natural finishes, inspired by Smith's visit to the nearby Gauteng bush land, also reflect the hotel's emphasis on sustainable, farm-to-table cuisine.

The dining spots are grouped on the hotel's sixth floor, at the base of a 200-foot-high, 20-story atrium that functions as a sort of upscale food court. A latticework canopy of walnut and stainless-steel beams shelters the bar and business lounge, instilling coziness while preserving sight lines. The architect even gave the landlocked space a view, not to mention a strong sense of place: Encircling the atrium just above the canopy is a photomural featuring black-and-white landscapes and portraits of South Africans.

Clockwise from below: A walnut partition housing books and TVs separates the librarylike business lounge from the bar, where communal tables foster interaction. Full-height glazing slides open for access to San Restaurant's outdoor dining area, with an ipe deck and fire pits. Lining the atrium is a collage of photographs shot locally. The entrance to Vin mmx allows a view of the central column studded with glass wine punts.

Three-meal restaurant, bar, fine dining, market and café, business lounge, open kitchen, and outdoor dining
Supporting the hotel's sustainable credo, the architect used only local contractors

PROJECT TEAM CASS CALDER SMITH, STEPHANIE KINNICK
ARCHITECT OF RECORD MDS ARCHITECTURE **INTERIOR DESIGNER OF RECORD**
BLACKSMITH INTERIOR INSPIRATIONS **RESTAURANT CONSULTANT** ADAM BLOCK
PHOTOGRAPHY ALFRED LOR
www.ccs-architecture.com

Standard

TOMMY BAHAMA LAGUNA BEACH
BAR AND GRILL + RETAIL STORE, CALIFORNIA

5,500 sf
100 seats

From top: *Carbonized-hickory shutters lend texture and dimension to the restaurant, whose walnut chairs and barstools have woven-leather seats; the lounge near the ceramic-clad bar features a vintage Pakistani wool rug and linen-covered sofa. Shutters recur in the retail area.* ➤

Tommy Bahama epitomizes laid-back coastal living: Think playful dresses, iconic men's shirts, and relaxed sportswear in cool, easygoing linens and cottons. Hired by the brand to design a hybrid shop/café in Southern California, Standard copartners Jeffrey Allsbrook and Silvia Kuhle captured that breezy island style by channeling a modernist beach house.

The space is on the ground floor of the city's historic Heisler Building, right across the street from the ocean. Patrons enter an airy dining area clad in traditional Bahamian wood-slat shutters, whose hickory planks have been heat-treated to mimic the coloration of teak. Shutters

also wrap a sofa in the lounge, screen off the restaurant's kitchen, and face bar cabinets. The motif reappears in the adjacent shop, where swiveling partitions are used to reconfigure the sales floor. This retail zone is elevated 18 inches above the dining area, a design nod to residential decks and the boardwalk nearby.

White-painted wood-beam ceilings and blackened-steel metalwork further unify the two zones, as does a sustainable ethos. The custom walnut furnishings were fabricated locally, and industrial paints and sealers were eschewed in favor of natural finishes, such as the plaster hand troweled on walls and tung oil rubbed into tabletops.

PROJECT TEAM JEFFREY ALLSBROOK, SILVIA KUHLE, KAZU SHICHISHIMA, BRANDON BOWN, JENNY LY

PHOTOGRAPHY BENNY CHAN/FOTOWORKS

www.standard-la.com

Clockwise from top:
Custom blackened-steel chandeliers illuminate the 100-seat dining area. Movable hickory partitions define the retail area. A hickory-and-steel ramp links the concrete-floor restaurant to the shopping zone.

1 ENTRY
2 LOUNGE
3 BAR
4 RESTAURANT
5 KITCHEN
6 RETAIL

0   10   20   40

Dirk Denison
Architects

FOODLIFE, CHICAGO

Food courts are generally multi-chain affairs, arraying high-fat choices around a sterile, brightly lit vastness of tables and chairs. Enter Foodlife, an urbane eatery in Chicago's Water Tower Place offering 14 options in surroundings that are unified, comfortable, efficient, and decidedly fresh.

Prior to its makeover, the 20-year-old, frequently remodeled mezzanine of the mixed-use high-rise was visually cluttered and, due to abundant hard surfaces and minimal insulation, aurally challenged. Dirk Denison Architects devised a plan that could be implemented in phases while the space remained open to the public. The result is an easily navigable and conversation-friendly experience. Sound-softening acoustic panels, mounted both horizontally and vertically, create a rhythmic pattern across the ceiling. Each color-coded serving kiosk features clean lines, coordinating finishes, and clear graphics—a scheme that carries through even to the drink, service, trash, and recycling stations. Etched-glass partitions delineate seating areas, imparting an airy feel. The lighting is kinder and gentler.

For takeout, there's a grab-and-go section and a bakery. Upon arrival, hungry dine-in guests receive a special card allowing them to select items from any number of kiosks—barbecue, pasta, tacos, sushi—and pay only once. It's the perfect solution for families, groups, or anyone who enjoys kappa maki with her pulled pork.

PHOTOGRAPHY MICHELLE LITVIN
www.dirkdenisonarchitects.com

Clockwise from above: Made-to-order salads are among the 14 dining options. Kiosk designs emphasize the presentation of food. Etched glass separates seating areas. Acoustic ceiling panels provide graphic texture, with vertical baffles and horizontal planes that change in relation to seating groups and ductwork. Guests dine in Claudio Dondoli and Marco Pocci's stackable polypropylene chairs or booths that offer banquette-style coziness. Flooring is ceramic.

XIE XIE, NEW YORK

Therese Virserius Design

Although she's now based in New York and caters to a primarily upscale clientele, Therese Virserius launched her design career at Ikea, in Shanghai. Well versed in Chinese culture—and in creating wallet-friendly style—she was the ideal choice to envision celebrity chef Angelo Sosa's Asian street-food restaurant, Xie Xie (pronounced *shay shay*, it means "thank you" in Mandarin). Located in the Hell's Kitchen area of Manhattan, the pint-size eatery was also conceived as a brand prototype, with design signatures that could be adapted to other locations. Given a tight budget and an even tighter footprint—just 400 square feet—Virserius got creative with low-cost but high-impact finishes: gradient-patterned facade signage, vibrant violet and chartreuse paint, graphic stripes that sweep from wall to ceiling, and a Corian-top counter faced with backlit panels of purple acrylic. A whimsical feature wall covered in candy-color fortune cookies succinctly sums up the design concept: tasteful, fun, and sweet.

400 sf
$150,000 budget
20 seats

PHOTOGRAPHY MELISSA HOM
www.theresevirseriusdesign.com

Clockwise from opposite: Stripes of violet paint run up a side wall and across the ceiling. Acrylic pendant lights cluster above the rear service counter. Opposite the counter is an installation of cast-porcelain fortune cookies glazed in Xie Xie's signature shades of chartreuse, violet, raspberry, and orange. The countertop is Corian; floors are wide-plank walnut.

TPG Architecture

EATALY, NEW YORK

For a moment, forget about the star power (including a certain flame-haired chef) behind this shrine to Italian cuisine. Don't give a thought to the five restaurants, wine bar, coffee shop, gelato vendor, and rows of artisanal foodstuffs beneath its roof. Contemplate instead Eataly's sheer size: 45,000 square feet spread across a single floor in New York's landmarked 1913 Toy Building.

TPG Architecture collaborated with the B&B Hospitality Group—owned by Mario Batali and Lidia Bastianich—and Italian businessman Oscar Farinetti, who launched Eataly in Turin in 2007, to develop a design that seamlessly fused dining with retail. The firm opted for an open layout interwoven with individually branded storefronts—set off by color or material—that showcase the art of food making. Thus restaurants sit cheek-by-jowl with the sprawling marketplace, which offers the very same pastas, olive oils, meats, cheeses, and other delicacies on their menus. Lifestyle elements, among them a cooking school and outposts of an Italian bookstore, bank, and newspaper bureau, make Eataly a one-stop shop for la dolce vita.

Entwining the many functions into a single space was a logistical challenge; so was revising the building's cast-iron facade to add new entry points. To comply with Landmarks Preservation Commission requirements, TPG re-created original details from archival photos. The designers took a similar tack with the interior. Period-appropriate floor-to-ceiling marble slabs clad walls, and a hand-laid "sugar cube" mosaic carpets the floor. Both play on the traditional Italian marketplace's look while also enhancing it for a new era.

Clockwise from above: Rows of spun-aluminum pendants illuminate Manzo, Eataly's most formal offering. Culinary options abound in the general sales area. Manzo's open kitchen lets customers watch chefs at work. A stack of wood used to fuel the bread-baking oven also functions as a design element.

45,000 sf
7 restaurants

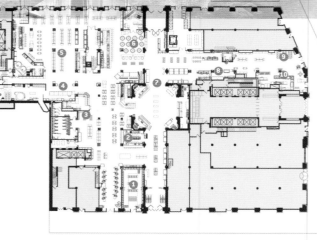

PROJECT TEAM FREDERIC STRAUSS, ALEC ZABALLERO, DIANA REVKIN,
VLAD ZADNEPRIANSKI. EATALY: CARLO PIGLIONE

PHOTOGRAPHY ALEC ZABALLERO/TPG ARCHITECTURE

www.tpgarchitecture.com

0   20 40   80

1 WINE STORE

2 LA VERDURE

3 BOOKSTORE

4 BREAD

5 PASTA

6 MANZO

7 PIZZA

8 PANINI

9 CAFÉ

10 GELATO

Clockwise from opposite: Adjacent retail and dining areas are floored in concrete. The space features classic food-hall touches like marble walls and terrazzo flooring. Industrial-style track lighting is augmented with pendants that break down the scale of the vast space. At vegetarian eatery La Verdure, Kartell stools pull up to a marble-top mosaic bar. Artisanal jams and olive oils fill shelves in the marketplace.

GrizForm
Design Architects

MANDU, WASHINGTON, D.C.

This Beltway eatery's sprightly design bridges cultures and generations. A native of Korea, the chef and her two American-born children requested a contemporary environment suited to enjoying such fare as soba noodle salads, spicy bibimbap, and pork bulgogi—but that didn't feel, per the younger clients, "too Asian."

Accordingly, GrizForm's decor gives familiar Korean elements a witty tweak. Dividing the dining area and bar is a partition made of oak "memory boxes," modeled on those used to house artifacts in ancient Buddhist temples. Stacked seven high in a metal frame, the boxes rise behind a long banquette to screen the mezzanine above. A dramatic ribbon of scrap-wood composite that extends from floor to ceiling evokes a bamboo forest. The element starts as a carpet near the entry, then wraps up the back wall and folds over to form a canopy. And the woven fabric covering the banquette mimics rattan, a material commonly used in Far East furnishings.

Emphasizing the high ceiling is a flock of carved-wood ducks, painted grass green to match the chairs and columns. This feature holds meaning for both generations: Popular in Asian eateries, the avian motif is also a nostalgic nod to the duck pond near where the chef's kids grew up.

Clockwise from above: A mezzanine seating area surveys the loftlike dining room. Neon signage on the glazed facade announces the café, whose name means "dumplings." The oak "memory boxes" have metal details. Suspended from the scrap-wood canopy is a series of woven lighting pendants. Roadside gabions inspired the caged-rock wall treatment that composes the partition's lower half.

2,800 sf
$850,000 budget

PROJECT TEAM GRIZ DWIGHT, MICHELLE BOVÉ, BROOKE LOEWEN
PHOTOGRAPHY PAUL BURK PHOTOGRAPHY
www.grizform.com

2,300 sf
60 seats

DH Design Studio

ALPINE HOUSE, PARK CITY, UTAH

Canyons, the largest ski resort in Utah, recently underwent a multimillion-dollar renovation that included the addition of a new base gathering area, 300 acres of terrain, the most technologically advanced chairlift in North America, and six restaurants. Among the latter is Alpine House, an upscale eatery that serves lunch and après-ski to private club members and dinner to the general public.

Hired to transform a raw space into a welcoming all-day dining destination, DH Design Studio was challenged by a strict footprint, limited budget, and 90-day turnaround. To save square footage, the firm combined the entrance and waiting areas and separated the resulting space from the dining room via a subtle level change and a metal-faced partition. An ice trough integrated into a floating bar chills beverages for waiting patrons. Once a table opens up, guests are led into the main space, which is clad in reclaimed barn wood accented with gold leaf. Seating upholstered in tones of red, gold, and green imbues warmth, as does an onyx bar and handmade brick accent wall. A mix of unfinished wood tables and banquette seating accommodates a variety of party sizes. And a feasting table with benches and sculptural tree-stump stools sections off the rear lounge, where diners linger in wingback chairs by a soaring metal hearth—très après-ski.

PROJECT TEAM REBECCA BUCHAN, MICHELE WHEELER, MATT DICKAMORE
PHOTOGRAPHY PETER AARON/OTTO (1, 4, 5), TESSA LINDSEY (2, 3)
www.dentonhouse.com

Clockwise from opposite top: The lounge sits adjacent to the bar, which features an underlit onyx counter. Squares of gold leaf embellish walls of reclaimed barn wood throughout. Above nailhead-studded ottomans in the wait bar is a mural of the Canyons property, hand-painted by the chef's father. Oversize burlap pendant lights hang from nonstructural ceiling trusses designed to hide mechanical and HVAC elements. Built-in printmaker-style bookcases—flanking the fireplace in the rear lounge—house accessories and conceal audio-visual controls.

DW Design Workshop

INK ICE CREAM, CHUNGLI CITY, TAIWAN

Talk about a cool concept: Icebergs in the Polar Sea sparked the slick white-on-white design of this Taiwanese ice-cream parlor. The glacial forms proved an apt metaphor—and not just because of the obvious chilly connection. "Each iceberg has its own personality, a distinctive way of interacting with its environment," explains firm principal De Shun Wang. That site-adaptive characteristic made the crystalline formations particularly applicable for this project, which would serve as a blueprint for future locations.

The "iceberg" here is the open kitchen anchoring one side wall. To accommodate a tight construction schedule, the designers chose a prefab solution rather than a custom one. The kitchen's swooping lines also help camouflage an existing I beam that projected obtrusively into the space. A cluster of five globe-shape pendants cast a wavelike pattern of light and shadow on the ceiling and floor, evoking the feeling of floating in frigid Arctic waters. The fixtures were carefully positioned to provide a modicum of privacy for diners in the second-floor mezzanine. A focal wall—dotted with a trio of clocks mounted on the diagonal—draws the eye up, inviting patrons to explore the secluded aerie. It features a continuous seating banquette and a steel balcony with clear glass panels...all the better to observe the swirl of activity below.

Clockwise from right: Three clocks near the open-plan kitchen reference the place of origin of the shop's main ice-cream flavors: Los Angeles, Taipei, and Rome. An enveloping L-shape banquette spans the length of the second-floor mezzanine. The existing concrete ceiling was texturized to contrast with the otherwise sleek surfaces. Above the kitchen is one of the original I beams that the designers worked into the new decor.

PROJECT TEAM CHING FENG LI, DE SHUN WANG
PHOTOGRAPHY KYLE YU
www.dwdw.co

1,250 sf
40 seats

PROJECT TEAM REBECCA BUCHAN,
MICHELE WHEELER, MATT DICKAMORE
PHOTOGRAPHY PETER AARON/OTTO
www.dentonhouse.com

Clockwise from top left: The outdoor patio serves food year-round. Overstuffed button-tufted wing chairs pull up to marble-top bistro tables in the private wine room, lined with 62 lockers for members' bottles. Wood ceiling beams, built-in cabinetry, and residentially inspired furnishings lend a loftlike ambience to the upstairs screening room. The exhibition kitchen's black-and-white ceramic-tile backsplash mirrors the dining room's painted-wood floor; wood columns lend a homey touch.

This boutique restaurant is something of a hybrid. It functions as a public dining destination as well as a tool to promote the Talisker Club, a family-friendly residential community set on 14,000 acres of prime Utah landscape. Located on the town's historic Main Street, the restaurant—formerly a real-estate and information center—is next door to the club's sales gallery, an adjacency that lets deal making segue smoothly from office to entrée.

Spread over two floors are four distinct spaces, all featuring a 1920s café theme. The main level houses a bright and airy dining room with painted checkerboard floors, pressed-tin ceilings, vintage light fixtures, and striped awnings. Outside is a gated cobblestone patio aglow with fire features and festoon lighting. A secluded wine room at the rear displays the restaurant's inventory alongside leasable glass-front lockers for storing members' private collections. Creating an authentic grotto feel are stacked-stone walls and hand-cut Italian roof tiles used to form groin and barrel vaults. A screening room upstairs isn't for watching Sundance flicks; it's where sales staff meet with prospective clients. This relaxing aerie mimics a residential loft with such touches as comfy seating vignettes and a photo-lined wall reminiscent of a family snapshot gallery. We're sold.

DH Design Studio

TALISKER ON MAIN, PARK CITY, UTAH

3,200 sf
93 seats

nightlife

Luckily for night owls, nocturnal culture has evolved well beyond the taverny watering holes and gimmicky dance clubs of yore. This cocktail-centric category has become more nuanced and sophisticated—not to mention culinarily cutting edge.

Designers are now charged with envisioning restaurants that lure a special breed of after-hours diner, cater to private parties, and otherwise keep the buzz going late into the night. Often that means creating flexible, multitasking layouts complete with no-holds-barred private zones and VIP areas (consider Twenty Five Lusk's "makeout" rooms) or chameleonlike spaces that segue from lunchtime casual to evening sultry (note Steel's mercurial decor). Elements that encourage interaction are de rigueur: DJ booths, communal tables, languorous seats that foster repose. (Using wine or liquor bottles as decorative details helps get people in the mood, too.) Of course, bars and clubs remain a favorite destination for revelers, although an ever-savvier clientele has designers upping the ante with inventive, changeable elements that keep patrons coming back for more. *We'll drink to that.*

JARDIN DE JADE RESTAURANT, HANGZHOU, CHINA

PAL Design Consultants

Walls abloom with abstract flowers, arty koi swimming across shimmery chandeliers, space-age clusters of salmon-colored pods—one peek inside this clubby restaurant and you know you're in for a treat. That was precisely the effect desired by the client, who tapped PAL to craft a novel design that would lure China's fast-growing population of young consumers hungry for unusual dining experiences. In short, the project brief was to dazzle.

An enigmatic layout goes a long way in accomplishing that goal. The aforementioned pods—which house VIP areas—create a meandering spatial flow that enhances the drama. (Their complex curves, however, posed a significant challenge to the construction team.) Rather than group these private spaces at one end of the cashew-shaped floorplan, the designers sprinkled them throughout, breaking down the lofty volume of the main dining area to more-intimate clusters.

The client also wanted the decor to read as Chinese without relying on clichés. Thus a pair of design motifs that lend local flavor. Pod walls are dotted with abstract blossoms modeled on Osmanthus, the official city flower. A warm glow emanates from oversize lighting pendants in the same four-petal shape. Other fixtures have aluminum-bead shades patterned with the sinuous profiles of koi, which are also found on metal screens in the main dining area. Courtesy of these stylized touches, the mood is subtly Asian—and unmistakably global.

12,900 sf
462 seats

Clockwise from top left: Lighting fixtures in private dining rooms were modeled on the petals of Osmanthus flowers, known locally as guìhaú. The blossoms also inspired metal sculptures on the pod exteriors. Walls of one pod peel away to reveal wine racks behind glass; flooring throughout is Nero Bello and Silver Black marble. Guests dine in leather chairs. ➤

0 10 20   40

1 ENTRY

2 MAIN DINING

3 PRIVATE DINING/VIP AREA

4 WINE ROOM

5 KITCHEN

Clockwise from above: *Circular columns are clad in a mosaic of bronze and mirrored tiles. A diner's-eye view of the petaled chandelier. Playfully curved portals leading to private dining rooms repeat the swoopy theme. Four colors of aluminum beads were strung together to create the chandeliers' aquatic pattern.*

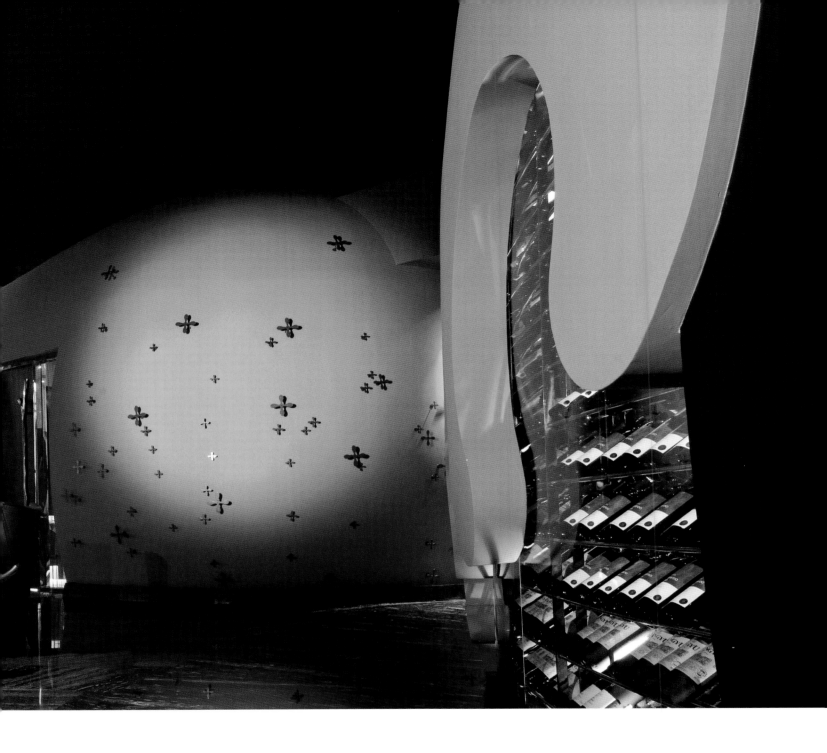

PROJECT TEAM PATRICK LEUNG, DORIS CHIU

PHOTOGRAPHY BAO SHI WANG

www.paldesign.cn

CCS Architecture

TWENTY FIVE LUSK, SAN FRANCISCO

Once home to a smokehouse and meat-processing facility, this 1917 warehouse has been transformed into a bi-level restaurant and bar serving New American cuisine and stiff drinks (firm principal Cass Calder Smith recommends the Dark and Stormy). The reworked brick facade inaugurates the see-and-be-seen vibe: Enlarged street-facing windows and a new frosted-glass entry offer teasing views inside. The voyeuristic mood continues in the dramatic double-height foyer, which provides a view of the restaurant a half flight up and the clubby lounge below.

The two spaces are stitched together by way of an angular white-plaster catwalk leading to the dining area, where it morphs into a low wall. For seating, Smith deployed a mix of banquettes and Pullman-style booths, as well as Macassar ebony tables that cantilever from the plaster partition. While nibbling on chicken-fried quail and grilled prawns, diners can watch chefs cooking in the glass-walled exhibition-style kitchen or survey the subterranean lounge, where leather sectionals surround stainless-steel fireplaces suspended from the ceiling via 20-foot flues. For more privacy, guests can book the 40-seat event room downstairs—or canoodle in the bunkerlike former meat-smoking areas, now semiprivate "makeout" rooms.

Clockwise from top left: Custom built-in seating lines both sides of the lower-level "makeout" rooms. The double-height lounge is warmed by alcohol-fueled hearths. Its underside visible from the lounge, a Venetian-plaster catwalk funnels guests from entry to dining area. The Macassar ebony tabletops of the dining booths slice through the low plaster wall, topped with stainless-steel plate. ➤

9,800 sf
$3.5 million budget
265 seats

1 ENTRY/CATWALK

2 MAIN DINING ROOM

3 CHEF'S TABLE

4 EXHIBITION KITCHEN

5 SEMIPRIVATE DINING ROOM

6 BAR

Clockwise from left: *Sleek polished plaster and stainless steel contrast with the structure's concrete and exposed-brick finishes and original Douglas fir beams. The 14-seat semi-private dining room upstairs features chairs upholstered in faux leather as well as laminate-glass artwork by Melissa Werner depicting abstract images of smoke. The restaurant is located in the former Ogden Packing and Provision building in the city's South of Market neighborhood. The main dining area, with leather-upholstered banquettes and booths, culminates in a bar faced in backlit glass.*

PROJECT TEAM CASS CALDER SMITH, BRYAN SOUTHWICK, BARBARA TURPIN-VICKROY, MELISSA WERNER

PHOTOGRAPHY PAUL DYER

www.ccs-architecture.com

Steve Leung Designers

SING YIN CANTONESE DINING, HONG KONG

Situated on the ground floor of the W Hong Kong hotel, this inventive eatery seduces locals and tourists with artful interpretations of the pulsing cityscape. In the soaring entryway, visitors encounter a stabile of traditional Chinese artifacts and graphic black-and-white signs suspended alongside photomurals of a busy street. The installation takes advantage of the lofty ceiling, which lowers to a cozier level in the restaurant proper. Steve Leung solved this structural challenge by playing up the tight confines. A passageway to the dining room re-creates the hustle-bustle of local markets via eating nooks designed to look like clothing boutiques, bookstores, and grocery kiosks. It terminates at a bank of fish tanks (a play on the ubiquitous Chinese restaurant fixture), incorporating LCD screens to interlace real and virtual aquatic life.

The main dining area can be divided into two zones, with full-height wall panels that indicate the theme of each: Central Skyscrapers and Kowloon Skylines. (The backlit images also distract from the dearth of windows and natural light.) In the VIP room, depictions of fishing villages channel the picturesque New Territories countryside. By dramatizing the contrasts that are Hong Kong's trademark—gleaming buildings and busy markets, pastoral parks and historic structures—the designer infused each section of Sing Yin with its own character, evocative of the humming urban life just outside.

PHOTOGRAPHY VIRGILE SIMON BERTRAND

www.steveleung.com

Clockwise from left:
Lining the corridor to the main dining area, semiprivate nooks pose as shops in a busy marketplace. Angled glass partitions separate colorfully lit semi-private dining areas. Photographic murals mark the Central Skyscrapers section of the dining area; the mirrored ceiling and carpet are patterned with a stylized map of Victoria Harbor. A cascade of birdcages enlivens a dining nook. Black-and-white signs and Chinese artifacts decorating the entry crystalize a sense of place.

4,014 sf
112 seats

THE MONKEY BAR, NEW YORK

BWArchitects

During the Great Depression, the Hotel Elysée's bawdy, smoky piano bar was *the* place to be in New York City, attracting artists, luminaries of stage and screen, and the era's top literary talent. Hand-painted murals, executed in the early 1950s by caricaturist Charlie Wala, gave the Monkey Bar its name; still on display, they depict sassy simians mixing cocktails, riding elephants, and engaging in other hijinx.

Over the years, alas, the spot fell into decline and faded from public memory. In collaboration with client Graydon Carter, the high-profile editor in chief of *Vanity Fair,* architect Basil Walter reinvented the saloon, updating its glamorous, speakeasy style with bespoke touches. Everything from the zebra-print rugs and leather banquettes to the long L-shape oak bar is custom. An artisan was hired to sculpt primate-shape table lamps that were then cast in bronze. And illustrator and cartoonist Edward Sorel painted the mural that now wraps the restaurant proper, depicting Jazz Age legends who once frequented the tony watering hole.

Since reopening, the Monkey Bar has again soared in popularity. Visitors dine on classics like clams casino, oysters Rockefeller, and lobster thermador under the watchful gaze of monkeys. Times have changed, though— the menu now offers the following prohibitions: No smoking, spitting, swearing, or pamphleteering.

1 RECEPTION

2 BAR

3 MAIN DINING

Clockwise from left:
Mirrored columns
divvy the restaurant,
whose perimeter
booths are raised
slightly above the
central seating area.
In the bar, the original
namesake mural has
been joined by
updated flooring,
new leather booths,
and simian-theme
sconces. Renderings
of the east elevation
of the bar and
restaurant.

3,500 sf
173 seats (restaurant)

PHOTOGRAPHY BILYANA DIMITROVA (1, 5), ROBERT CAPLIN PHOTOGRAPHY (2–4)

www.bw-architects.com

G+
Gulla Jonsdottir
Design

HYDE, LOS ANGELES

Sunset Strip revelers are used to getting the once-over before making their way past the velvet rope. But Hyde does that convention one better. A glowing pair of come-hither eyes gazes out from a windowless facade painted the color of dusk. The seductive peepers, veiled by a lacelike steel mask, beckon you to a pitch-black door a few feet away. Good luck gaining entry: You've stumbled onto Hyde, one of Hollywood's most exclusive hot spots.

Edgy hospitality developer SBE tapped Gulla Jonsdottir to overhaul the five-year-old lounge's decor. The client requested a more open layout but otherwise gave the architect carte blanche. Working with a $600,000 budget and a six-month timeline, she gutted the space, starting from scratch with the goal of creating a soft jewel box.

Jonsdottir achieved that goal with a design that pits hard against soft. Clubgoers pass through a filigreed tunnel sculpted from recycled rebar. The lounge beyond is similarly enveloping (if a bit more cosseting), lined with champagne-hued leather scales. Roving lights behind them animate the room with flickering shadows. Semicircular booths span both sides of the space, which culminates in a bar decorated with jagged wood boxes and incorporating a gem-like DJ booth. The bijou theme extends even to libations: Bubbly is served in crystal jewelry boxes.

0 5 10   20

1 ENTRY

2 VIP BOOTH

3 MAIN LOUNGE

4 DJ BOOTH

5 BAR

Steve Leung Designers

INAKAYA, HONG KONG

7,535 sf
189 seats

After 40 years based in Tokyo, the legendary restaurant Inakaya opened a Hong Kong outpost on the 101st floor of Kowloon's International Commerce Center. To reflect both its Japanese origins and new location, Steve Leung chose a traditional sake brewery—with a modern twist, of course—as his theme to guide the interior decor.

The interplay of old and new is introduced in the lobby. Patrons enter a hallway furnished with a sculptural brewing tank and lined with canted sake barrels supported by a metal frame. Graphics of trees etched onto glass walls set an autumnal tone, as does a ceiling canopy embellished with stainless-steel abstractions of leaves. In the sleek bar beyond, guests enjoy harbor views through windows fronted with open shelving. After drinks, they move on to the atmospheric main dining room, where spherical glass pendants illuminate a Zen-like sea of dark marble and wenge. The space is full-on contemporary Japanese, delineated by movable shoji screens. There's also a *teppanyaki* counter plus a *robatayaki* area tricked out like a Japanese residence with a granite cobblestone path, ceramic roof tiles, timber latticework, and *noren* fabric panels. For more privacy, book one of two VIP rooms. Their ceilings are patterned with *temari* "thread" balls, a favored hostess gift and good-luck token—and a crafty offering of best wishes to visitors.

Clockwise from opposite: A brewing tank and stacked rows of sake barrels animate the entry. Geometric wood screens distinguish the teppanyaki area, where a raised platform allows diners to take in the view. The wenge-clad entry doubles as a wine library. Cross sections of wenge form an earthy feature wall.

PHOTOGRAPHY VIRGILE SIMON BERTRAND

www.steveleung.com

TPG Architecture

LA BIRRERIA, NEW YORK

Clockwise from top: A new steel structure supports a retractable canopy of insulated polycarbonate sandwich panels. A glass storefront wall separates the brewing room from reception. The concrete staircase leading to the roof level is painted with Italian phrases. Below custom brass pendant lights is the 32-seat bar, topped with Carrara that was skirted to create the illusion of a thicker slab.

After opening the sprawling Italian food marketplace, Eataly, on the ground floor of a historic Manhattan high-rise, the Batali & Bastianich Hospitality Group took additional square footage on the penthouse and roof levels to create an indoor-outdoor cask-ale brewery and restaurant. The project had its challenges. Because the building is a designated New York City landmark, a full-size mock-up of the proposed addition had to be erected using tarps and poles to confirm that it would not be visible from the street. Later, it turned out that few cranes in the vicinity were capable of lifting the steel onto the roof, and the process required a busy block of 23rd Street to be closed for an entire day.

Visitors, however, have an easier time getting to this festive aerie: A dedicated elevator at Eataly goes straight to the 14th-floor reception, carpeted in hard-working end-grain mesquite. A wall of black iron and glass with glazed transoms offers views of copper brewing vats beyond. The rooftop bar is a long stretch of Carrara marble. Tables feature salvaged wood, while the deck consists of staggered planks of faux bois porcelain tile. Late in the design process, the clients asked for a retractable roof, to allow winter use of the boxwood-ringed deck. Good thing: The space, as it happens, is packed year-round.

PROJECT TEAM FREDERIC STRAUSS, ALEC ZABALLERO, VLAD ZADNEPRIANSKI, DIANA REVKIN.
B&B HOSPITALITY GROUP: LISA EATON

PHOTOGRAPHY MARK LA ROSA

www.tpgarchitecture.com

6,000 sf
150 seats

Dreamtime Australia Design

STEEL BAR & GRILL, SYDNEY

This restaurant owes its unusual blend of industrial and organic chic to a wager between Dreamtime's founding principal, Michael Mc Cann, and his 10-year-old daughter, Michelena. After she declared him unable to design anything "that wasn't brown," a bet ensued. If his next restaurant project had even a speck of brown, she would win. And that was not Mc Cann's only challenge. The all-day eatery also needed to feel light and airy during breakfast and lunch yet downright sultry at night.

Dad won the bet, while still hewing to a minimalist palette. Steel's decor—a silvery admixture of metal, glass, waxed concrete, and gray-stained timber—lives up to its name. Stainless steel predominates, appearing everywhere from the mosaic-tile loos to the 9-foot-high mesh partitions divvying the dining area. A central open kitchen provides the dramatic focal point, with its polished plate-steel firewood rack, Brazilian granite countertop, and vent hood treated to mimic aluminum foil. Various back-of-house features are glass-enclosed for diners' amusement, such as a produce refrigerator and an elevator between the kitchen and basement storerooms. There's also a wine cellar backed by an internally lit sculpted mirror—actually an art installation by local architect Dale Jones-Evans.

The heavy-on-the-metal design extends to the outdoor dining area and cocktail lounge as well. An enfilade of silver-wire pole lights sprout from the communal table. Aluminum fans swirl overhead. Stainless-steel mesh faces the walls. And cagelike cocktail tables house egg-shape lights. You could argue that the sandstone bar front breaks the "no-brown" rule but, fortunately for her dad, Michelena had deemed beige an acceptable alternative.

Clockwise from above: Partitions of polished stainless-steel mesh have niches for displaying artworks. In the private dining room, warmed by a sand-blasted sandstone fireplace, is a 13-foot-long custom pendant light in silk and stainless-steel wire designed to resemble a glowing cocoon. The raised deck is faced with Calacatta marble. Sandblasted sandstone also clads the gray-stained-timber deck's bar. ➤

Clockwise from opposite: In the stainless-steel-mosaic bathrooms, mesh-enclosed vanity pedestals house ovoid lights and swivel mirrors have inset flat-screens that play music videos. In the middle of the main dining area, a custom glass elevator descends to the basement prep space. Open wine racks span one wall. Near the stainless-steel-plate firewood storage, a glass-walled cool-room showcases colorful produce; abstract appliqués animate the cement feature wall at rear.

4,000 sf (interior)
950 sf (deck)
16 weeks to complete

PROJECT TEAM MICHAEL MC CANN, SOO SING CHANG, TIM BARRY, POONAM RANDEV, ALISHA REA

PHOTOGRAPHY PAUL GOSNEY

www.dreamtimeaustraliadesign.com

1 DINING ROOM
2 KITCHEN
3 BAR
4 OUTDOOR DINING
5 RESTROOM

Therese
Virserius Design

BAR VDARA, LAS VEGAS

Housed within the Vdara Hotel & Spa, this Sin City hangout was designed to work hard and play hard. By day, it's a bright, cheerful coffee bar; at night, the indoor-outdoor space morphs into a sophisticated and decadent lounge. And thanks to flexible elements like modular seating, a four-sided bar, and drop-down flatscreen TVs, the hot spot can simultaneously host myriad activities—from musical performances to sport nights—and accommodate walk-ins and private parties at the same time.

Credit this multitasking design to Therese Virserius. Her vibrant scheme made the most of architectural challenges such as an odd eye-shape floorplan. She also grappled with a lack of solid walls; now, a row of 16-foot-tall curved rosewood partitions screen Bar Vdara from the hotel's public areas. A similarly porous boundary serves to distinguish indoors and out. Glass panels, built-in planters, and champagne-hued sheers mark the dividing line while preserving views and openness.

Furniture in punchy hues was chosen with kicking back in mind: low-back lavender barstools, cushy English wing chairs decked out in orange upholstery, sofas strewn with graphic pillows inspired by candy wrappers, and settees whose tufted backs are embroidered with fuchsia peonies. But as the sun sets and the drinks sink in, the terrace's whimsical daybed-like swings—built for six—become the most coveted seats in the house.

4,700 sf
$6 million
budget

Clockwise from top:
Upholstered garden swings hang from braided ropes. Modern interpretations of an English wing chair furnish the lounge. A sculptural woven-metal chair on the terrace. The perimeter of Bar Vdara is traced by a rosewood portal and screens; sheers curtain the glass between indoors and out.

PHOTOGRAPHY ERIC LAIGNEL
www.theresevirseriusdesign.com

PETER AARON / OTTO
www.ottoarchive.com

BEN BENSCHNEIDER
www.benschneiderphoto.com

ROBERT BENSON
www.robertbensonphoto.com

VIRGILE SIMON BERTRAND
www.virgilebertrand.com

MAGDA BIERNAT
www.magdabiernat.com

RICHARD BRYANT
www.richardbryant.co.uk

PAUL BURK
www.paulburkphotography.com

ROBERT CAPLIN
www.robertcaplin.com

BENNY CHAN / FOTOWORKS
www.fotoworks.cc

NIALL CLUTTON
www.niallclutton.com

JIMMY COHRSSEN
www.jimmycohrssen.com

CHRIS COOPER
www.chriscooperphotographer.com

CHRISTOPHER CYPERT / CYPERT AND LEONG
www.chriscypert.com

BRUCE DAMONTE
www.brucedamonte.com

BILYANA DIMITROVA
www.bdphotography.com

PAUL DYER
www.dyerphoto.com

KAT FILIPINAS
www.katfilipinas.com

RYAN FORBES
www.ryanforbesphotography.com

FRANZEN PHOTOGRAPHY
www.franzenphotography.com

MARC GERRITSEN
www.marcgerritsen.com

PAUL GOSNEY
www.elbow-room.com.au

ART GRAY
www.artgrayphotography.com

JEFF GREEN
www.jeffgreenphoto.net

KEN HAYDEN
www.kenhayden.com

MELISSA HOM
www.melissahom.com

EVAAN KHERAJ
www.evaankheraj.com

MIKIKO KIKUYAMA
www.mikikokikuyama.com

MICHAEL KLEINBERG
www.michaelkleinberg.com

NIKOLAS KOENIG
www.nikolaskoenig.com

photographers
index

INTERIOR DESIGN®

editor in chief Cindy Allen

EXECUTIVE EDITOR
Elena Kornbluth

DEPUTY EDITOR
Edie Cohen (West/Southwest)

ARTICLES EDITOR
Annie Block

SENIOR EDITORS
Mark McMenamin
Deborah Wilk

MANAGING EDITOR
Helene E. Oberman

ASSOCIATE EDITOR
Meghan Edwards

DESIGNERS
Zigeng Li
Karla Lima
Giannina Macias

BOOKS EDITOR
Stanley Abercrombie

EDITOR AT LARGE
Craig Kellogg

CONTRIBUTING EDITORS
Aric Chen
Laura Fisher Kaiser
Raul Barreneche
Nicholas Tamarin

PRODUCTION MANAGER
Sarah Dentry / 646-805-0236 / sdentry@interiordesign.net

DIGITAL IMAGING
Igor Tsiperson

RESEARCH DIRECTOR
Wing Leung / 646-805-0250

REPRINTS
Ness Feliciano / 708-660-8612 / fax 708-660-8613

INTERIORDESIGN.NET
WEB EDITOR
Laurel Petriello

ASSISTANT WEB EDITOR
Ashley Teater

DESIGNWIRE DAILY CONTRIBUTORS
Ghislaine Viñas
Ian Volner
Larry Weinberg

SANDOW | MEDIA™

chairman and ceo Adam I. Sandow

CHIEF FINANCIAL OFFICER AND CHIEF OPERATING OFFICER
Chris Fabian

VICE PRESIDENT, CREATIVE AND EDITORIAL
Yolanda E. Yoh

VICE PRESIDENT, INFORMATION TECHNOLOGY
Tom Cooper

president Mark Strauss, hon. iida

ASSOCIATE PUBLISHER
Carol Cisco

DIGITAL MEDIA DIRECTOR
Pamela McNally

STRATEGIC AD DIRECTOR, NEW YORK
Gayle Shand

MARKETING DIRECTOR
Tina Brennan

EVENTS DIRECTOR
Rachel Long

ASSISTANT TO THE PRESIDENT
Kalyca Rei Murph

MARKETING
ART DIRECTOR
Denise Figueroa

SENIOR DESIGNER
Mihoko Miyata

SENIOR MANAGER
Yasmin Spiro / 646-805-0287

INTERIORDESIGN.NET
DIGITAL MEDIA MANAGER
Ashley Walker

GO-TO BUYERS GUIDE PRODUCER
Eric Perl

SERVICES
BOOK SERIES DIRECTOR
Selina Yee

HALL OF FAME DIRECTOR
Regina Freedman / 646-805-0270

CONTRACTS COORDINATOR
Sandy Campomanes / 646-805-0235

SPECIAL PROJECTS MANAGER
Kay Kojima / 646-805-0276

SALES
SALES REPRESENTATIVE
Kathy Harrigan / 646-805-0292

INTEGRATED MEDIA SALES
Karen Donaghy / 646-805-0291

INSIDE SALES DIRECTOR
Jonathan Kessler / 646-805-0279

SALES ASSOCIATE
Xiang Ping Zhu / 646-805-0269

SENIOR SALES COORDINATOR
Valentin Ortolaza / 646-805-0268

PHILADELPHIA
Greg Kammerer / 610-738-7011 / fax 610-738-7195

ATLANTA BUYERS GUIDE, E-SALES MANAGER
Craig Malcolm / 770-712-9245 / fax 770-234-5847

CHICAGO
Tim Kedzuch / 847-907-4050 / fax 847-556-6513
Julie McCarthy / 847-615-2077 / fax 847-713-4897

LOS ANGELES
Reed Fry / 949-223-1088 / fax 949-223-1089

FRANCE/GERMANY/POLAND
Mirek Kraczkowski / kraczko@aol.com / 48-22-401-7001 / fax 48-22-401-7016

ITALY
Riccardo Laureri / media@laureriassociates.it / 39-02-236-2500 / fax 39-02-236-4411

ASIA
Quentin Chan / quentinchan@leadingm.com / 852-2366-1106 / fax 852-2366-1107

AUDIENCE MARKETING SENIOR DIRECTOR
Katharine Tucker